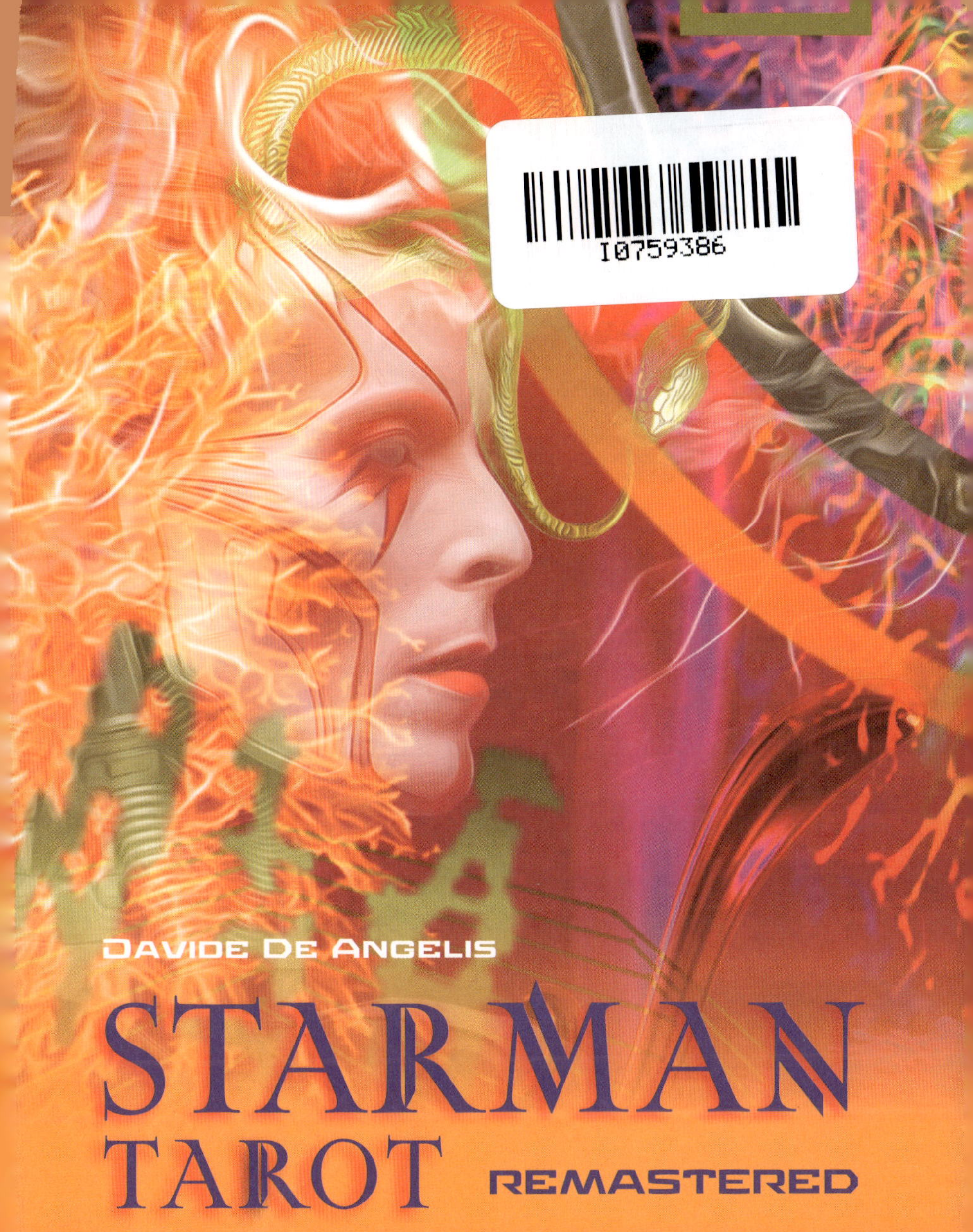

DAVIDE DE ANGELIS

STARMAN TAROT REMASTERED

4880 Lower Valley Road, Atglen, PA 19310

Library of Congress Control Number: 2025930160

Designed by Danielle D. Farmer
Cover design by Danielle D. Farmer
Type set in Map Roman/Aviano Future/Adobe Caslon Pro

ISBN: 978-0-7643-6990-2
Printed in China

10 9 8 7 6 5 4 3 2 1

Published by REDFeather Mind, Body, Spirit
An imprint of Schiffer Publishing, Ltd.
4880 Lower Valley Road
Atglen, PA 19310
Phone: (610) 593-1777; Fax: (610) 593-2002
Email: Info@redfeathermbs.com
Web: www.redfeathermbs.com

CONTENTS

WELCOME TO THE *STARMAN TAROT—REMASTERED*

There is a saying, "Choose extraordinary goals because of who you will need to become in order to realise them."

The *Starman Tarot* was indeed an extraordinary goal, yet, paradoxically, I cannot fully claim to have chosen it. The deck called me forth from a space that existed just beyond the veil of logical reasoning. It flowed into my consciousness with a scintillating energy, highly visceral, electrical, deeply emotional; a kind of directive formed from symbols and feelings. I clearly understood that this Tarot deck wanted to be radiantly alive, to be a presence in the world that truly touched, moved, and inspired people to discover the underlying beauty and magic of reality, gifting fresh visions and perspectives to explore—live—and to thrive as a result.

The feedback I have received, now from thousands of people across the world, since its original launch in 2018, has centred around this very tangible sense of aliveness, energy, colour, and light frequencies that are evoked as people work with the cards. My mind has literally been blown by some of the messages I've received from people sharing their experiences of using the deck. They range from those who have been inextricably guided to their soul partner, with marriages magically rekindled and saved, to amazing projects catalysed and brought to fruition. Floundering businesses have been transformed into successful ventures, with people directed to powerful paths of physical and mental healing, and some even embodying the significance of the *Starman Tarot* in their lives through physical tattoos. The most profound communication, though, being someone who shared how working with the *Starman Tarot*—and the deep, heartfelt content within its book of guidance—prevented them from taking their own life.

Sceptics may ask, how is all this possible from images printed onto pieces of card? All I can say is that the experiences people share are very real and meaningful. Our logic-dominant culture, with its set of values, beliefs, symbols, and assumptions, always seeks to shape, organise, and categorise that which it deems useful. While extremely helpful, logical reasoning and prediction leave little room for us to be moved by the deeper, more miraculous, nonphysical, and mysterious beauty of Nature.

These messages and communications from people using the *Starman Tarot* have both deeply touched my heart and confirmed the energy I myself feel when creating and working with the deck. Many times, I have been gifted very different ways of understanding reality, moved to trust my intuition and expand my vision, feeling a higher frequency of life energy moving through my physical, emotional, and spiritual essence.

On one occasion in 2023, despite it being a beautiful late summer's day, and life being pretty good, I was nevertheless experiencing waves of anxiety and felt shadowed by a cloud of low-level depression. I remember glancing down at the *Starman Tarot*

deck that always sits on my desk. Two cards were separated out; the Nine of Swords and the Sun. Uncharacteristically, I didn't bother to give this much of my attention and simply placed them back and closed the box. Soon after, I went for a walk in a very lovely and dramatic piece of nature known as Durden Downs near my home in Bristol, UK. As I walked out across a field of lush grass, the sun suddenly became utterly iridescent. A staggering array of vibrant colours, deep, rich golds and oranges, alongside beatific rays of violet, radiated from its core. I looked around to see if other people had noticed; it seemed so startling, surely something must be happening? To my surprise, everyone was just going about their business as usual, people jogging, others walking, eyes glued to their phones.

As I continued to watch this astonishing light show, I became entirely enveloped by a vast presence of peace and wonder. Free of attachment, I noticed the stream of fearful and negative thoughts arising from the dark recesses of my mind; a sense of life being pointless mixed in with old fears, hurts, shame, and regrets. It seamlessly came to me that this was the message of the Nine of Swords—to see clearly all the fear and pain that we needlessly carry through life, and to observe that these painful streams of thought are not who we are. Instead, they arise completely of their own accord, patterns of energy that the mind attaches meanings to. After so many years of psychological and spiritual exploration, I already understood this intellectually, but to see it playing out so clearly, so crisp, apparent, and visual, was incredibly liberating.

As each unpleasant thought arose, it was cleansed or, more accurately, lovingly dissolved by two spiralling helixes of golden light. And very gradually these two golden spirals of light became physically manifest in front of me. A soft yet immensely powerful communication flowed forth from them, gifting me understandings of the spiritual reality of light and plasma—the intelligence and miracle of light and plasma. It was as if—for just an instant—I saw into the "Mind of Light"— En-*Light-in-Ment*. I could intimately "feel" the sun speaking to life. I remembered my daughter, when she was three, seeing sunlight reflected upon the sea and saying, "Light speaking to water." I felt so joyful and free! Free of perceived burdens. I understood in that moment that light speaks and plays with flesh, blood, and bone—as electrons flowing through the body, a dynamic dance between ourselves and the rest of the world, people, trees, rivers, buildings, animals, clouds.

This incredible expansive state of consciousness and awareness remained for several days. I instinctively knew it would fade, but, strangely, felt no sadness. In the glow and radiance of this heightened state, an image of a beautiful Sun Goddess blossomed into my imagination, the new rendition of the Sun card. This is how light intelligence guides us to create. I look forward to you meeting her in this remastered deck.

So, as I welcome you to this remastered *Starman Tarot*, know that the aliveness, the energy that I speak of, has once again moved me to work on the cards. The call was to adjust and evolve the deck to enhance the communication of each card and the communication of the deck as a whole entity.

Alongside the evolved artworks, it was also the right time and opportunity to reimagine this book of guidance and respond to the practical feedback from people using the deck, and to make some important adjustments, such as the size of the cards for greater ease of shuffling and enhancing the quality of the materials. I am truly feeling the exhilaration of this new creation journeying out into the world, embarking on fresh adventures, connections, possibilities.

In this time of instant AI "art," I feel it is important to emphasise that this deck was in fact decades in the making. A significant number of elements woven into the deck were originally created by hand (drawn, written, painted) or had their origin very much in the analogue world (personally photographed and manipulated), collected over many years and only latterly rebirthed in digital forms. Each minute detail was carefully considered and placed in its rightful position by me alone. At times, it was incredibly difficult, yet equally exhilarating because I could feel the energy guiding my actions.

In this Remastered *Starman Tarot*, every new element has been gifted the same care, focus, and inspiration to fulfill its resonant purpose. These new elements now live and contribute to the thousands of hours of creative endeavor, the evolution of artistic and philosophical ideas I explored whilst working with David Bowie—and all the incredible energy/effort and focus that it took to truly realize the *Starman Tarot*. Ultimately, impactful art, infused with history, focused intention, and meaning, created via the energy and dexterity of a living human nervous system, carries the very tangible aliveness that so many people have felt when working with this deck. AI, no matter how sophisticated, cannot feel the energy and emotion or traverse the life experiences and potent connections that infuse a work of art, an idea, with tangible, living presence. The *Starman Tarot* remains, and shall forever remain, enriched with this "living" presence.

I wish you a truly wonder-filled experience. Over many years of exploration, I've come to know that we are increasingly moving into a time when we can explore the realm of "the impossible"—the reality of what we don't know that we don't know. We have many amazing systems, wisdoms, and instruments to help us on this journey. I strongly believe that the *Starman Tarot* and its ability to bring new vistas of wisdom and powers of guidance to "light" through the system of the Tarot is part of this emerging energy. So, in this spirit of adventure and magick, may this *Starman Tarot—Remastered*, serve as an inspiration, a wise and powerful cocreator for you to live fully expressed, finding the most creative, loving, and productive path through your challenges. May it move you joyfully toward your greatest triumphs, turning your life into a beautiful work of living art.

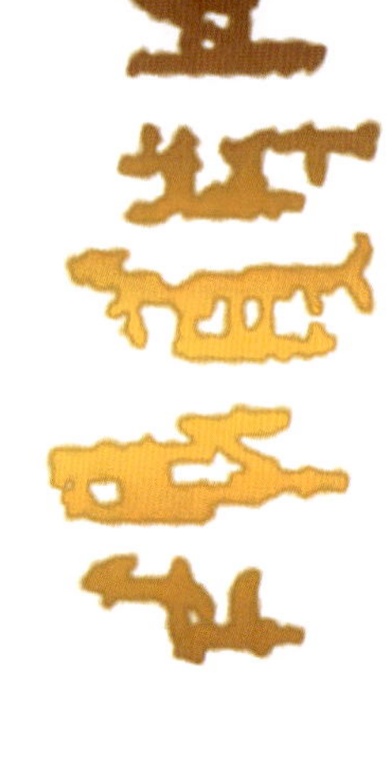

JOIN THE ADVENTURE

If you would like to discover more-inspirational ways to explore the Tarot, to greatly enhance your life energy, vital health, and creative power to naturally manifest beauty and living abundance, then I invite you to join us on the adventure. Visit my website at www.davidedeangelis.com.

DAVIDE DE ANGELIS

BRISTOL, UNITED KINGDOM

THE JOURNEY

I have an unshakable belief that I was guided to bring the *Starman Tarot* to life. It absolutely wanted to exist! At the same time, so many diverse elements had to unite just to fashion me into the right person to finally create it, to respond to its desire to manifest. It seems that I had to be taken apart and be put back together several times before arriving at the optimal version of creativity, technical skill, knowledge, and life experience to do the work as it needed to be done (for now). It wasn't always plain sailing. And when I say "for now," I'm referring to the "living energy" of the deck and how it may ultimately always be evolving toward yet-unknowable spectrums of expression.

In this way, the *Starman Tarot* is an emergent phenomenon, artistically potentialised by my collaborations with the iconic David Bowie. Combined with my aching desire to explore and visualise the nature of reality, it has given birth to rich and complex forms of graphic art—"potent visual alchemy" as Bowie described it.

ART AND VISION

The process of creating art, when united with a powerful vision—a directive, galvanises an expansive energy and acts as a catalyst to express something meaningful. A form of alchemy—visual alchemy—is birthed. I spoke about this many times when working with Bowie, and it was central to everything we did together. The meeting of art and directed vision gifts us the opportunity to view our lives and the world through more-wonder-filled eyes. When using the *Starman Tarot* and other visionary systems, we are granted a vaster viewpoint of our life and the dynamics that shape our destiny. Our situations and circumstances, no matter how surface flawed, are alchemised into the raw materials that give birth to higher potentials.

In a strange twist of life and time, the energy of the cards spans across forty-years, arching back to my first-ever encounter with Bowie in the early 1970s, while traversing the many years of my searching, questioning, and honing the knowledge and disciplines of ancient and futuristic mystery schools. I have lived, practised, and experienced the nature magic of shamanic traditions, psychedelics, yoga, meditation, lucid dreaming, and astral travel; the study of consciousness, philosophy, psychology, music, and sound healing; and even the pain and bliss of ultra-endurance sports. All of these are visually and energetically woven into the fabric of the *Starman Tarot*.

Into this weave we must add the joys and frustrations of all the artistic projects I've put my heart and soul into creating throughout the years, the numerous places across the world that have shaped and influenced my experience, the beauty and richness of living with my young family in Bali, and finally the reluctant return to the legend-soaked grit and earth of the southwest of England.

The cards resonate with the amazing, accomplished people I've met and the rich, tangible experiences and opportunities that transpired as a result of working with

Bowie. The cards are infused with the energetic imprint of the team of incredibly talented designers that worked together with me to bring creative projects to life. My then business partner Derek Scanlon, who also brought his meticulous sense of design detail and integrity to several of the Bowie projects, helped set the stage and hold space for the creative innovations that caught Bowie's eye and drew him to connect in the first place. Looking back, I can now clearly see that everything that came to pass simply had to happen. The inspirational highs, successes, and innovations; the disputes; the seemingly chaotic decisions, alongside my often-reckless refusal to compromise the art even a tiny fraction, to spare myself and others from massive amounts of struggle and inconvenience.

THE ETHEREAL FIGURE OF BOWIE

Tracking all the way back . . . It was a late at night when the rapier-thin, ethereal figure of Bowie walked into the Italian restaurant my dad managed in Old Compton Street in London, I was just ten years old. The restaurant was a mere stone's throw from the now-legendary Trident Studios where *Ziggy Stardust and the Spiders from Mars* was recorded. Bowie and his companion, with brown, shoulder-length hair and a smart suit, were quickly ushered to the back, away from the glare of attention. I found myself sitting directly opposite their table. I'd been drawing, kind of tired and a little bored, waiting to go home. Suddenly, I was right in the epicentre of something! My dad told them I was his son, but almost before the words left his lips, Bowie's gaze zoomed in on the paper I had been drawing on, his attention hovering above the newly sharpened HB pencil sitting beside it. In a gentle, slightly dreamlike manner, he asked if he could borrow them. Time seemed to span out. The smoke from his freshly lit cigarette wafted nonchalantly across the room. I remember how that pencil and paper became giant in my attention. I fumbled slightly as I handed them over. Convinced he needed to make some important notes . . . I wasn't sure they were fit for purpose. Instead, looking as if he had just found the answer to some unimaginable question, Bowie set about adding to the already strange drawing I'd been absently working on. After downing his drink and lighting another cigarette, he courteously handed the drawing back as both men left in somewhat of a hurry, flowing gracefully past tables and out into a waiting car. Only then did I look at the drawing. It reminded me of something primitive, a cave drawing. I still have it to this day. Look out for it woven into the deck.

THE OUTSIDER

Little could I have imagined that twenty years later, I would once again find myself sitting beside Bowie, pencil in hand, drawing on a piece of paper. Only this time, we were visualising ideas for the dystopian world, populated by Outsider artists and mythological creatures for his album *1-Outside*. This was to be another significant change of direction for Bowie, and he wanted something disturbing—cutting—yet

infused with hypnotic, otherworldly beauty. It marked him reuniting with Brian Eno and working in an intensely experimental and improvisational way. Evolving from the William Burroughs cutup technique employed by Bowie to create lyrics in the '70s, this time a computer program called Verbasizer was used. This randomisation theme would become key to how we approached a large part of the artwork. More than just a cover and some notes, Bowie wanted to create a storybook around the theme of the album and expand this across fine-art pieces and installations. In other words, the designs needed to be thought of as something that would work across a multitude of different platforms.

Given all the possible paths through life, how on earth did I come to be working with David Bowie? Having seen some experimental design and typography that I had featured in a design magazine called *Creative Technology*, Bowie literally phoned me directly to ask if I would be interested in working with him to create the design and images for his next album. The call caught me completely off guard; it took me a few moments to believe that this was in fact David Bowie. This call sparked a time of radical transformation for me. One moment a struggling, experimental designer, the next I'm working with a creative icon, with a world stage on which to perform a unique, artistic show. I can say, hand on heart, that if someone had asked me back then who would I most love to collaborate with on creative projects, without a nanosecond's hesitation it would have been Bowie!

Every aspect of the artwork in this Tarot deck aims to capture the energy and essence of our kaleidoscopic relationship with life and spirit: maps of consciousness. It is multicultural, multidimensional, mysterious, strange, and provocative. I present this as an ongoing relationship between the will of Nature, the ancient mystery schools, the system of Tarot, the artistic energy catalysed by my work with Bowie, and you, the user of the *Starman Tarot*. I offer it as a powerful and dynamic tool to help you live your fullest creative expression.

THE POTENCY OF DRAMA

Working with Bowie on the albums *1-Outside* and *Earthling* and a wide spectrum of artistic projects, I learnt how to infuse design and art with the potency of drama: Bowie was a master at this. In my honing this vital skill, each image in the *Starman Tarot* arrives fully formed and at the same time constantly shape-shifting across time, just as we also change and transform. Exploring our relationship with time is a theme that follows me through everything I create. Bowie, when looking at a design or even a piece of typography, would ask me what happened before and what happens next? In an age of constantly moving images, the ancient craft of manifesting an entire dynamic reality just from a still image evokes our imagination in a unique way. The *Starman Tarot* aims to do just this. Every card plays out as a complex microdrama with the capacity to change according to how you view it.

The artworks for the *Starman Tarot* traverse the art forms / mediums of experimental typography, street art, eroticised sci-fi imagery, influences of Caravaggio and the

Renaissance, chaos theory, philosophy (in particular, Socrates, Plato, Pythagoras), shamanism and plant medicines, the destroyed imagery of punk, sacred geometries, and the art of some of the earliest Tarot decks such as the Sola Busca. The Starman of this deck and many other characters also pay homage to Jack Burnley's original 1940s superhero Starman.

In the artworks I created with Bowie, I would often be drawn to the Japanese art of kintsugi—the art of repairing broken pottery with gold, silver, or platinum. I'm totally fascinated by the process of transforming something perceived as damaged or even ugly into something of increased beauty and value. Many of the cards in this deck began life as images that I had created over the years, increasingly manipulated and "distressed" until the intrinsic beauty contained within was revealed. A seemingly random piece of typography suddenly became an entire environment in which a character could exist. This is a form of delight that comes out of the creative process. Working artistically with Bowie gave me lavish opportunity to practice kintsugi with typography and photography alike. Many of the backdrops for the *Starman Tarot* cards began life as something completely unrelated: an unremarkable, faded photograph of a building, which when constantly manipulated by hand and computer would reveal a magical realm in which to place one of the deck's archetypes. The sheer appropriateness of what was revealed through these seemingly random acts would often appear utterly miraculous to me. A whole new reality sitting behind the world we directly encounter: the extraordinary hidden within the ordinary. At times it became clear to me that the fact that we can change into something else is a form of salvation. Life will of course automatically do this—it is a process of constant change, but how much more empowering for us all if we can participate; be the one adding, subtracting, or inverting something in our life to reveal a new form of knowing, doing . . . being.

THE JAPANESE ART OF KINTSUGI

The card visuals often express a playful, trickster nature: the sky made out of the earth and earth made from sky, in the same card. There are mirror images that reveal something normally hidden. Solid ground is not where you may expect it to be. I play with the elements of earth, water, fire, and air and how they are expressed through the

environments and characters in the deck: a normally earthy archetype can be found floating in air, but it may not be what it seems at first glance. This is part of my own nature woven into the cards and the enjoyment of anthropomorphising the deck, letting it play with me, read me, challenge me—who is actually creating what? I wanted there to be a natural, rebellious joy to this Tarot deck to counterbalance the serious issues it must also traverse. And all this before the dramatic entrance of AI. It makes me smile when I now receive messages asking what AI I used to create the cards. All the hours spent agonising over where to place even the tiniest element, sitting into the night, staring until I thought my eyes would bleed. But this is the energy it called forth to carry the right resonance and frequencies out into the world at this time.

THE ARTISTIC SEEDMOTHER

The artistic Seedmother of the final cards can be traced directly back to the ideas for a Tarot deck I started conceptualising in 1995 when working with Bowie. As a central theme, the archetype of the Starman was so alluring to me. I've had a lifelong fascination for the art of Tarot, and the possibility of fusing the creative ideas I explored with Bowie, with the potent, visually rich symbolic system of the Tarot and other wild mythologies, was the ultimate opportunity and challenge: My artistic and psychological destiny is one way I can look at it. Strange as it may sound, I've felt that a Tarot deck has been following me ever since I was a small child; though I was barely able to conceive of such a thing, it was inviting me to create it. And yet, I couldn't quite see it until I started working with Bowie.

I thought the time was ripe back in 1995 to forge ahead, but I quickly discovered that it wasn't an easy matter to put perhaps more than a solid year to one side, in order to fully realise such a project. However, I was able to see clearly that the mysterious deck following me had been waiting for the right artistic fusion before wholly revealing itself. Since then, what I instinctively called *Starman Tarot* has been a very tangible presence. As the years rolled by without me getting down to serious work, its quiet invitation to be born steadily morphed into a full-blown demand!

I was living in Bali when I heard the shocking news that Bowie had passed away in January 2016 at age sixty-nine, two days after the release of his twenty-sixth and final album. An intense incident that took place around a week before was perhaps a herald of what was coming. It was late morning as I was returning home with my daughter, Solaria, from our local juice bar. An epic-looking tropical storm that had seemed to be in the distance suddenly loomed overhead. Eager to avoid the drenching and pyrotechnics, we decided to cut across a narrow path that snaked precariously through a small rice paddy. Several locals had already taken cover under tiny huts that snuggled close to the path. We had made it about halfway across when we were dazzled by a colossal sheet of lightning that parted to present us with a writhing ball of creamy light plasma, the size of a football, travelling toward us on the path. Everything happened in an instant; time slowed to a crawl. Quicker than thought, I instinctively pushed Solaria to one side as I could do nothing but watch the voltaic ball roll along toward us, before exploding several feet away in a deafening crescendo that shook the

earth under our feet. In its seismic wake, I became aware that the people sheltering under the huts were praying. Mercifully, everyone was absolutely fine, apart from the shock and ringing in our ears from the bang. Incredibly, Solaria, who was only four, remained completely unfazed, looking around in fascination at the people praying. I too closed my eyes and gave thanks for our safety and respect for the power of Nature. Many ancient cultures understood a lightning ball or fireball to be the essence of a messenger spirit whose appearance signalled that a death of some influence was imminent. I didn't have to wait long to find out the answer.

The two nights following Bowie's passing, I experienced a series of intensely vivid dreams in which I was actually holding the *Starman Tarot* deck. I was fanning through it, seeing the cards clearly. When I told my wife, Esther, she said that I simply had to put everything else to one side and realise what I was meant to do. However, there was just one majorly important issue: The cards in my dreams were even more intricate and rich with references than I had previously visualised. As a fellow creative, Esther (as did I) knew that such a project would demand a huge commitment of resources, time, and energy, but even armed with that knowledge, after a year of working around the clock, seven-day weeks, we started naming it the artistic Iron Man—a pun on the gruelling race that can finish off even the most-determined and fittest athletes. Almost every card has traversed several attempts to stay true to the cards that downloaded into my dreams. This remastered deck now moves yet closer to that ideal.

EXPLORE AND QUESTION

As you may have already guessed, this Tarot deck is not about repeating what is already known and shared about Tarot. There are many others far more capable than I who are already doing that. Instead, the *Starman Tarot* serves to ignite something; it seeks to explore and question through the power of creativity. Every card offers a fragment of life examined from a specific context. From my perspective, the Tarot is a phenomenal system to help us craft a life truly worth living. The cards serve as very powerful "lenses" that we can view life through and seek answers and direction.

This book of guidance is written with my amazing wife, Esther De Angelis. Together we have taken life on and lived through a commitment to share what we have learnt and are still learning—to shower life with the possibility of radiance, wonder, and beauty. Her input into the creation of the *Starman Tarot* cannot ever be fully expressed in words. This book is a combined effort—an intimate collaboration, a sharing of love, courage, beauty, and passionate commitment to offering something powerful and transformative.

Each card asks you to live in the questions it poses, and to experience something for yourself. It calls for you to be your own teacher and guide: You are the one you've been waiting for! In the explanations contained in this book, we are not trying to write great literature or claim that we possess anything that anyone else doesn't inherently have access to. Apart from the obvious Bowie influences, *Starman Tarot* contains a multitude of other artistic, cultural, historical, philosophical, and mystical references

and symbols. Esther and I have tried to give you a pungent taste of each card, along with the character traits, teaching, and learning from each archetype and different characters, but we didn't want to reveal everything and, in so doing, strip away the delight of discovery and the allure of mystery. For this reason, I believe that the *Starman Tarot* has the capacity and potency to travel with you through time, constantly revealing new parts of itself, and new facets of you. You will get to know it, and it will get to know you.

Some of the cards were extremely difficult and rebellious characters to deal with. I had to fight with them. These fights were mostly dirty and undignified. Sometimes they flatly refused to yield their innermost secrets and kept me struggling to gain sight of their true nature. The art threatened to push me to the breaking point on many occasions. But somehow, paradoxically, those breaking points were also sublime. Even now, every time I look at those difficult cards, even with this remastered deck and greater understanding, I feel their symbolic eyes on me, confronting me with questions. In remastering the deck, I have once again connected with these powerful archetypes and asked them to reveal more of their character and directive. Ultimately, I came to understand that the struggles and uncertainties are in fact the sign of something vitally alive, unwilling to compromise just for the sake of completion. I have often looked at the process of creating the deck, bringing the message and energy to fruition, as having to negotiate with my Daemon, or some spirit of fate, who is relentlessly focused on demanding I express every facet of creative potential. Everything "for now" is as good as it could possibly be, for now the Daemon and I have come to an agreement. The tussles I still have with some cards stay as a reminder that this will never be over for me, and only now can I welcome this and no longer feel the burden. A powerful Tarot deck, a powerful call and urge to create, is never passive in any way!

ASTONISHING REALMS

This entire *Starman Tarot* project is an elaborate collaboration. Looking back at all the people who have helped turn this into a reality, I simply have to sit in pure amazement. I bow down in humble thanks. It would not be right for me to pass over the opportunity of offering my gratitude and admiration to the team at Lo Scarabeo, who published the first version of the deck. And now through this amazing *Remastered* deck, my gratitude and admiration go out to REDFeather Mind, Body, Spirit and their dedicated team, for bringing such great enthusiasm, professionalism, and passion to this next exciting phase of the *Starman Tarot*.

The intense afterburn of working creatively with Bowie is still playing out both in my life and in the world. The designs and art I created during that time stay with me, a visual background radiation. Creating the *Starman Tarot* has guided me across many astonishing realms of possibility. It has lifted me to incredible highs and dragged me through some of the lowest and most difficult times. Just like a Bowie project, every phase of this Tarot's creation has been both an Odyssey and Oddity. This deck appears to me as a vital, living entity: a friend, a lover, an enemy, and goad, but ultimately a wise and powerful guide. It simply demanded to be created. It just so happens it

chose me for the job. In finally bringing it to life, just like Bowie, I had to become many different characters. It has transformed me and will continue to do so. I believe it will transform you too, in unexpected and positive ways.

If you are moved and inspired by Bowie, it will communicate strongly with you. If you are passionate about Tarot, I believe it has something powerful and meaningful to offer you. If you are a lover of art and the inherent quality of creativity, it will speak directly to you. And if you have a passion for natural magic, the great mystery schools, the nature of consciousness, the miracle of light, the complexities of design, and the weaving of inspirational stories and ideas, then . . .

I welcome you to the adventure of the *Starman Tarot*.

If you would like to discover more-inspirational and more-diverse ways to explore the Tarot, greatly enhance your life force, vital health, and creative power to naturally transform and reconfigure the energy of your own life so that you can manifest joy, beauty, and abundance in the world, then please join us on the adventure. Together as a growing community and tribe using the teachings and tools in this book, we can reshape and cocreate, changing the way we think and feel about ourselves and each other. We can act with renewed vitality, power, insight, and vision to change the world.

Visit: www.davidedeangelis.com

THE MYSTERY ORIGINS AND EVOLUTION OF TAROT

The Tarot is a dynamic, living system that has the capacity to communicate ideas, reveal possibilities, and guide you in mysterious and yet amazingly practical ways. To tell the story of how we have arrived at the Tarot that prevails today, we must walk a winding path where several narratives—true, false, and unknown—converge to deliver us to something of value (that runs on a fuel beyond logic). With this in mind, let's set forth on a journey that opens each fragrant petal of the Tarot into a map of consciousness, evoking ancient philosophies and practices, spiritual realms, vistas of imagination, and futuristic ontologies. I hope you enjoy the ride through history and mystery and let your own direct experience of working with the *Starman Tarot* and other well-crafted, energy-rich decks guide you to new heights and possibilities.

THE NEW WAVE

We are witnessing a new wave of interest in and fascination with the Tarot, and the art of the oracle, playing out around the world. They are finding their way into situations and domains that were previously unreceptive, even hostile. Many other intuitively powered systems, ancient and emerging, are also growing exponentially into our consciousness, transforming how we understand our connection to nature, our own inner nature, and the cycles of birth, death, and rebirth. These systems are also presenting us with new thoughts and ideas about how to create businesses and products, navigate our relationships, and pass value and wisdom on to the next generations.

The growth of the Tarot coincides with the seismic shift in our cultural relationship to psychedelic plant medicines and the fungi realms for healing ancestral patterning and exploring and expanding consciousness. The same is happening with our use of sound, movement, breath, and light to heal and enhance our vitality. The barriers are falling, as the willingness to honour the awesome majesty of these symbiotic relationships and teachers kindles a rebirth, or recognition, of our spiritual LIGHT nature.

Despite the disharmony, greed, fear, and terrible suffering that's happening and being documented in such ultravivid detail in our lifetimes, it is growing evermore clear that after millennia of dormancy, we are once again opening to the astonishing wonder and sacredness of life—the inseparable connection to something unimaginably vast and multidimensional. The rapture is rising as a higher frequency of experience grows stronger, and if we allow ourselves to become quiet, turn away, and cast aside the messages of doom, we can feel the current of something radiant, exhilarating—the currency of aliveness in a new way. Those who would strip this world of colour, texture, movement, beauty, and wonder, trapped in the holding patterns of power over and domination, are losing their once-iron grip. Their narratives and rhetoric sound hollow and ridiculous; we can see right through them. This new flourishing will continue to

grow and delight in every single being that invites it in, allowing it to enrich their words and actions with a fresh, vital energy.

THE REALMS OF IMPOSSIBLE

In times to come, as we transition from the age of Pisces into Aquarius in astrological terms, the consistent dissolving of old, dysfunctional mind patterns, belief structures, and ways to interact with reality that no longer serve our highest potential will unfold. An illumination of what has long been forgotten or previously impossible will increasingly become available.

From the fantastical possibility of communing with the hyperintelligent plasma clouds—the substance of souls—that hover between the earth and the moon, to entirely new facets of science guided by the miraculous realities of light, water, and magnetism. As we become receptive and ready, we will be gifted access to radically new levels of consciousness to explore and create with. What beckons those with a passion—a deep desire—for our human flourishing, and the beauty and sanctity of animals and all sentient creatures, is not a fusion with AI, but rather a union with what can be described as "spirit technology"—the light cognition of the god/goddess mind. We will understand that many representations of "conscious" technologies that appear to have come from ancient, mythological sources were in fact seeds from the future and other dimensional realms sent to grow and bear fruit when the time was right. Signals flowing back from the "Transcendental Object at the End of Time," as the ethnobotanist and mystic Terence McKenna suggested. All these radiant possibilities are woven into the artwork and symbolism of the *Starman Tarot*.

THE GUIDING PRINCIPLE

If we become sensitive and open to this guiding principle, we will be entrained . . . harmonised with its directive or greater will. This is essentially the shift from travelling through the fear-inducing, thought-run system of a separate ego, to a life that is spontaneously played like a living instrument. Our relationship to the mind and the intricate functioning of our bodies—blood, bone, electricity, flesh, neurons, melanin, and all the myriad movements—will also be compelled to shift and accommodate a higher frequency of existence. Our primary source of energy will come mainly from light not food, alongside a far-greater intensity of our body's endogenous light. Industries that fuel sickness and unimaginable cruelty will flounder and be replaced by foods and elixirs that naturally elevate our creativity and sense of well-being. These adjustments to our minds and bodies can already be felt emanating from deep within and all around. This is the alchemy; our lives with all their struggles and seeming imperfections are transformed into the raw materials that can be turned into the gold of a meaningful and artful life. Raw consciousness waking up to itself. But everything is a fine balance, a delicate dance. The astonishing potential for a New Earth remains mostly latent within these times of transition.

THE REIMAGINATION OF TAROT

The evolution or reimagination of the Tarot, infused with a powerful, creative-led functionality, has surfaced now to play a role in this next level of awakening, or new phase of consciousness: magick and mystical wonder, woven together with the faculty of logic, analysis, and computation. So, we have travelled through vast tracks of time, from a magical, unifying, and respectful relationship with "intelligent" life and into a logical, acquiring, analytical reality and are finally moving into a cocreative union of magic and logic to liberate an entirely fresh possibility for being human.

The evolution of Tarot will help us understand our lives from the vantage points of light, the archetypes, the symbolically potent realms, and patterning of mythology. In this evolution of Tarot and other magical systems, you gain access to the expansive sight of a visionary and the wisdom of a futuristic shaman, the Starman archetype. We will have the means to explore our lives from a higher vantage point, understanding the greater energetic impact of thoughts, beliefs, words, and actions. We can examine reality through the open questions that emanate from our interactions with a particular card and its associated archetype. The Tarot, alongside other creative systems of inquiry—some yet to manifest—will grant us enhanced insight alongside the courage to stand strong, face our fears, embrace the paradoxes, and even resolve them. Through working with the Tarot, we can consciously create the contexts in which our gifts and life potential are activated. False beliefs and limitations come into sharp focus, giving us the opportunity to choose with greater care and heart. It is the living of your potential—the expression of your creative spirit—that sits at the epicentre of the *Starman Tarot*.

THE HEART OF TAROT

Let us flow further into the adventure, uncovering the mystery, by exploring the origins of the actual word TAROT. On the surface, we are told that it sprang forth from the Italian "TAROCCHI," with its origin unknown.

If we care to seek outside the normal scope of information, it's as if the Tarot has cleverly concealed its true identity, energetic expression—purpose—within its very name, inviting us to delve, explore, and contemplate. Is it purely by chance that the word TAROCH was used as a synonym for foolishness in the late fifteenth and early sixteenth centuries, a time when it was indeed foolish to challenge the final authority of the church? Where better to hide wisdom and sources of magic than behind the hapless mask of the fool? And as we examine the full emergence of TAROT, other sources of wisdom, energy, and connections begin to emerge.

TORAH

The Torah, (biblical Hebrew: תּוֹרָה Tōrā), which means to instruct, to guide and teach. These instructions are the "Law" (old Norse root of the word "law," lég: to be "laid down"), given by sacred authority. The word "Torah" denotes the five books of Genesis, Exodus, Leviticus, Numbers, and Deuteronomy. In Christianity the Torah is known as the Pentateuch or the five books of Moses, the Hebrew prophet, teacher, and leader who received the ten commandments from Yahweh or God, the originating cause of everything. If you read the lettering at the centre of the Wheel card in the Tarot backward, you arrive at TORA. We have the opportunity to connect to the Akasha, the memory or imprint we carry inside about the past, present, and future.

TARA

Let us consider TARA, supreme goddess or female Buddha (awakened one). In the region of the Himalayas, especially Tibet and Nepal, she is referred to as the Wisdom Goddess, the embodiment of perfected wisdom and universal compassion, the ultimate "mother" who gives birth to the buddhas of the three times, as in Tārā Tantra—Dipankara Buddha, representing the past; Shakyamuni Buddha, representing the present; and Maitreya Buddha, the future. Tara can be seen as the "Mother TREE," the bodhisattva, bodhi (tree) sattva (quality of goodness, purity). Through her, the "Body of Goodness" is made possible. The name Tara is also translated as "cross" or cause to "cross over," as well as "savioress" or "rescuer." An interesting synchronicity when we view this in connection with the rise of Tarot as we "cross over" into the age of Aquarius.

TORUS

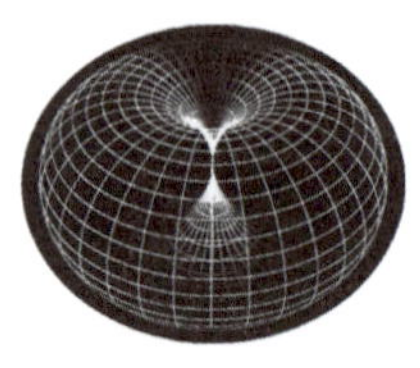

Then there is TORUS. In the realm of sacred geometry, the "torus" reigns supreme as the symbol of interconnectedness, the eternal flow of energy, and the delicate balance between the physical and spiritual worlds. It embodies the perpetual cycle of creation and destruction, birth and death, the very essence of existence, Nature's recurring masterpiece. This donut-shaped surface that's created by revolving a circle around an axis in three-dimensional space is said to underlie every atom, molecule, cell, and other larger structures in space. We radiate the torus field, the largest electromagnetic field around the body from our heart centre, in the middle of our torso. In the torus we can see the "creaTOR."

TAURUS

We move to TAURUS and the story of Zeus, Greek god of thunder and lightning, ultimate ruler, protector, and father of all gods, purveyor of law, inner illumination, and order, who fell in love with Europa (from whom the continent Europe was taken), the virgin princess of Phoenicia. Zeus turned himself into a miraculous white bull to seduce her, then cast the star constellation of Taurus into the heavens. Interesting to note that the Romans, following the Greeks, regarded their god Jupiter as the equivalent of Zeus, king of all deities, to form Ju-Zeus.

TRUTH

We then arrive at TRUTH. Tree and truth come from the same distant root. We can explore the connection with the Tree of Life, the knowledge of good and evil. Truth is seen as being in accord with reality, bearing no subdivisions. Various theories and views of truth continue to be debated among philosophers, theologians, and scholars in the process of trying to define truth as opposed to falsehood. Truth perhaps can be viewed as "what it is" and may be seen as the qualities of faithfulness, fidelity, and loyalty to a standard, honesty, sincerity, and veracity. For the ancient Greek philosophers Socrates and Plato, truth was an eternal, objective reality that could be approached through rigorous inquiry and philosophical reasoning. It was not merely factual correctness but a higher understanding that aligned with ultimate principles such as the Good. Pursuing this truth was essential for personal and societal well-being, making philosophy a vital path to living a meaningful life.

THOTH

And last for now, let's look at THOTH, the Egyptian god of the moon, patron of astrology and alchemy, credited with inventing writing and language, messenger of the gods. From Thoth we are gifted a fusion with the Greek god Hermes to give us Hermes Trismegistus (Hermes the Thrice Greatest), a syncretic creation, avatar being, that emerged out of the Hellenistic period and the conquests of Alexander the Great, to teach and author the Hermetica, the foundation of the philosophical system known as Hermeticism. This teaching gifted great wisdom of physical and spiritual reality, alchemy, astrology, and magic, later becoming treasured by alchemists and artists of the Renaissance alike in their quest for the great spiritual work. Searching for the Magnus Opus, the great work to create the Philosopher's Stone, the substance and symbol that represented divine illumination, heavenly bliss, and perfection. Believed to turn lead into gold, or "the tincture" used to make the elixir

of life, the Philosopher's Stone has never been found, and yet, the search for it led to the development of chemistry, metallurgy, and pharmacology. To this day, the debate as to the TRUE origin of the Hermetica rages on—you will discover its significance as we continue our journey with the Tarot.

THE SIGNATURE CODE

We can see from this brief voyage into the possible encrypted messages within even the word TAROT that in many ways, the phenomenon of the Tarot is far more fascinating, interwoven with powerful mysteries and interlaced paths that are seldom cited in most explanations. It steadily becomes clear that something greater, the signature code of an evolutionary intelligence, is at work . . . TAROT—TORUS—TRUTH.

It's fascinating and remarkable to note that beyond what we think the Tarot is doing or communicating, all the highly sophisticated philosophies, windows into human psychology, futuristic dimensions and artistic expressions, and a multitude of other complex interconnections and technological innovations needed to take place to manifest the deck of Tarot. This is all part of the magick, which encompasses and guides where it will go next, perhaps even beyond the digital? But how did we even arrive at something as innovative and revolutionary as the "technology" of a printed card that could powerfully communicate emotions, principles, and qualities? The roots of playing cards and card games likely lead back to long-lost civilizations and cultures that possessed untold abilities and modes of consciousness, now just energetic echoes in space and time.

THE ANCIENT ROOTS

We can trace the idea of throwing the knucklebones of sheep, pigs, or other small bones of quadrupeds to contact divine truth, brought to India from Africa about 40,000 years ago. Here we clearly see a record of interacting with something physical and symbolic to offer up "hidden" information.

The board game Senet, which was found in predynastic tombs in Egypt circa 3100 BCE and is beautifully depicted being played by the Egyptian queen Nefertiti herself in 1295 BCE on the walls of her tomb. Despite the original rules of game play being subject to conjecture, by the time of Queen Nefertiti, it had been conceived as a journey of Ka, the vital spark that leaves the body upon death, through various stages to the afterlife. Credited with her prominent role in changing Egypt's religion from polytheism to monotheism and the worship of the sun god Aten, the pieces represented human souls, with each of the thirty squares arranged in three rows having their own particular religious significance.

In ancient China we see the emergence of clay tiles (bone cards). These bone cards were in use for over a thousand years during the Tang dynasty, which at the apex of its flowering around 800 CE was the golden age of cosmopolitan culture. Their

paper counterparts certainly date to 1294, the Mongol Can dynasty, but all the peoples in the great continents of Asia and Africa have created remarkable games dating back thousands of years. All these facets can be seen as energetically interlaced, leading to increasingly complex ideas being shared through the form of cards.

However, it was not until late in the fourteenth century that playing cards found their place in European society, while the first documented Tarot deck, known as Triumph Cards, was described in the Italian court records of Florence. With its additional symbolic, philosophical, and poetic illustrations described as the Triumphi (trump cards) to the traditional four-suit pack of hearts (water), wands (fire), clubs (earth), and spades (air), their creators endeavoured to illuminate our most-complex dilemmas and desires. Most early decks of Tarot cards would have been wood-block-printed and hand-coloured with stencils, until the invention of the printing press by Gutenberg in 1440, revolutionising the dissemination of ideas through mass printing toward the latter half of the sixteenth century.

EXPANSION OF IDEAS

Finally, we arrive at the 1500s, and the Italian aristocracy enjoying a game known as "Tarocchi Appropriate," in which players were dealt random cards as thematic narratives for writing poetry for each other. These early cards strongly reflected the Christian world and its driving principles. However, the evolution toward a more powerful, divinatory usage soon became established, with particular artists' imagery used to evoke more-specific intentions, hidden patterns, and energetic transmissions that were understood only by an inner circle of people who were in pursuit of esoteric knowledge. We can understand how this fuller / more complex idea of the Tarot could flourish in Renaissance Europe, especially Italy and its birthplace, Florence.

The Renaissance, with its great arbiters Leonardo de Vinci, Botticelli, and Michelangelo, marked the transition from the Middle Ages to the Modern era, a period of some three hundred years from the fourteenth to the seventeenth centuries. It was a time that saw renewed interest and study of the cultural ideas of antiquity, fostering capitalism, diplomacy, and humanist educational reform and, above all, found expression in the arts. Italy, with its unique position of small city-states, supported new forms of social and political organization, no doubt spurred on by the turmoil that the Black Death plague caused in killing almost half of the population. It has been suggested that with so much death in the air, people's values changed, and much thought was given to life here on Earth rather than the afterlife. Upholding the virtues of fairness, justice, and liberty so conducive to academic and artistic support and development, the Renaissance birthed humanism and its focus on intellectual and physical excellence epitomised in the modern expression of Tarot.

THE TWISTING PATHS

As we move into the eighteenth century, there were so many more twists and turns in the path of the Tarot, so many elaborate inaccuracies and claims of heritage that have, unpredictably, in their own way, led to how we now work with the Tarot today. We will explore how some of the most significant people, mystery schools, and interpretations have woven a new vision of the Tarot together. Essentially, key figures, in possession of selected information, have, in strange and complex ways, opened doorways for unexpected wisdoms and meanings to find their way into the Tarot. It's easy to overlook how "Life" can use all kinds of methods to manifest what is most aligned to the direction of its imagination.

If you look back over your own life, it may become obvious how so-called mistakes and apparent false beliefs have moved you to grow, do important things, and arrive at a fresh understanding of who you are. We cannot have the scope of vision to know how the universe puts things together. In fact, if we apply what is called "computational irreducibility," the notion that the calculations needed are so great that only actually "living" in real time and then looking back can reveal something even close to an answer. The synchronicities and seemingly impossible or implausible things arising can make sense only from a certain point in the unfolding or manifestation. With any luck, we have that lightbulb moment and suddenly see how it all fits together. Having considered the idea of TAROT as a kind of cipher, can it really be a random, meaningless accident that events transpired to create such a rich bandwidth of knowledge and wisdom that is now the Tarot? The powerful interconnections and directives that appear out of the Tarot's journey through time cannot be explained, and yet, they somehow tap into the root of an unknowable universal will—this is a wonderful paradox, magick in action.

TIMELESS WISDOM

A very significant path in the evolution toward our modern Tarot can be traced to a publication of *Le Monde Primitif* (1778) by a Swiss Freemason, Antoine Court de Gébelin. Primarily on the basis of his "immediate perception," he posited that the Tarot was an arcane repository of timeless esoteric wisdom, indeed the very book of wisdom sometimes known as the Book of Thoth. De Gébelin interpreted the symbolism of the Tarot de Marseilles, the name coined by French card historian Romain Merlin. As you can see, such wonderful threads weaving together. Just taking a look at the name Romain Merlin, we get Romain, referring to a citizen of Rome, and Merlin, tracing back to Merlin Ambrosius Aurelianus, a warrior prophet who was said to be among the last of the Romans in Britain. This warrior prophet was later merged with Myrddin Wyllt, a "wild" figure in medieval Welsh legend to eventually become Merlin Ambrosias of the Arthurian legend. As we will see later, the energy of a legendary multifaceted magician, prophet, warrior, and saviour is so alive throughout the modern Tarot.

The Tarot de Marseilles points back to ancient mystery traditions such as those of the Egyptian goddess Isis (is is—it is that it is), connected to the idea of the Great Mother, magical healing. Important for our Tarot adventure, and the energy and message of the *Starman Tarot*, Isis is associated with Light. A sun goddess, she is celebrated in the Festival of Luminosity. Isis sees and "illuminates the other gods with the radiance of her light." There is also a connection to the star Sirius, meaning to sparkle or be lit. More and more we see this idea of shining light upon wisdom that's needed for a higher perspective or vision. De Gébelin also made reference to Osiris, the Egyptian god of fertility, agriculture, and vegetation, while also being the god of the dead, the underworld, and the afterlife. And here we come to the notion of "As above, so below," a way of understanding that was further woven into Western consciousness by the pre-Socratic Greek philosopher Anaxagoras, born around 500 BCE, and later more fully expressed in Plato's amazing dialogue *Timaeus* (360 BCE).

THE GREAT LIBRARY

Another important path in our journey is that De Gébelin fervently believed that the Tarot de Marseilles contained many coded references or even a distillation of the ancient wisdoms housed in the great Library of Alexander, accidentally destroyed by fire in 48 BCE by Julius Caesar during the civil war. Moving along this trajectory, we now witness this wonder-filled library, a depository of ancient sacred writings and chronicles finding its way into the future through a belief that its secrets are encrypted into a Tarot deck. This way of seeing the evolution and new emergence of the Tarot is truly magical. Once the idea is set in motion, some of the most valuable and vital teachings from the Old World, infused with vibrant legends and stories, become part of the Tarot's lexicon.

Importantly, there have been many versions and card makers of the Tarot de Marseilles. The first was possibly the work of Pierre Madenié of Dijon, France, created in 1709. He was a master card maker and engraver, but the exact origin of where he gained his inspiration is lost in the mists of time. Many skilled card makers had access to old manuscripts and references to long-forgotten mystery schools and traditions. Importantly, engraving plates were often passed down through generations, so the actual origin may be far deeper.

KNOWLEDGE OF ORIGINS

Ancient wisdom of the Old World—the knowledge of origins, of consciousness, of being—has made its way through time to manifest into the symbolic and archetypal forms within Tarot. This is clearly illustrated within the word "Arcana," with the Tarot divided into two distinct parts, the Major and Minor Arcana. Arcana is from the Latin, *arcanus*, meaning secret. Alchemists were said to be pursuing the arcana of nature and sought elixirs for transforming base metals into gold, prolonging life and curing disease. The frequent association of the word with the alchemists' elixirs influenced the use of "arcanum" for "elixir."

The first twenty-two cards of the Tarot are called the Major Arcana, and it can be said that these cards contain the major or big mysteries or secrets—Big Magic—Natural Law. This is a system of law based on a close observation of natural order and human nature, an ethical theory that claims that human beings are born with a predetermined moral compass that governs their behaviours and affords the equal right to live and the right to happiness. The Major Arcana is also often referred to as "trumps." Here again, we can fathom how secrets could be hidden from view, since it is derived from "se tromper de," to mock or act the fool. It's also pertinent that the Fool can be the one who dares to ask the difficult questions that challenge preconceived viewpoints and culturally accepted beliefs. In modern culture, this can go further by asking, "Who Am I?," "Who Are You?," and "What is Real?" The fool is also equated with the number "zero," which can be interpreted as "What I don't know, that I don't know"—the dark womb of creation/realm from which genius is sparked.

TWENTY-TWO

But let us track back to the number twenty-two. Our adventure now encompasses certain terms, beliefs, practices, and organizations with the introduction of a character called Éliphas Lévi Zahed (1810–75), a Frenchman whose original name was Alphonse Louis Constant. His professional name, Éliphas Lévi, was an anagram of his given names "Alphonse Louis" into Hebrew. Starting out in life as a would-be Catholic priest, he later became renowned as a revolutionary socialist, utopian visionary, artist, poet, and, above all, author of several highly influential books on magick, occultism, and magical freemasonry.

The three chief components of Lévi's magical thesis were Astral Light, the Will, and the Imagination. The latter two components were proposed centuries before by Paracelsus (Swiss physician, alchemist, lay theologian, and philosopher of the German Renaissance), an original seeker of universal wisdom influenced by the Hermetic, Neoplatonic, and Pythagorean philosophies, which were central to the Renaissance. So many strands of knowledge and lived experience passed down through generations, crucial to the flow of influences infusing the Tarot. In her book *The Secret Doctrine*, Madame Helena Blavatsky, cofounder of the Theosophical Society in 1875, called Lévi "the most learned, if not the greatest of the modern Kabbalists." Although, along with others, she was later far less flattering/complimentary when saying that "no other Kabbalist has ever had the talent of heaping one contradiction on the other."

Regardless of his ultimate knowledge and authority, for sure, as we will discover, it is largely thanks to Lévi that the Tarot is so widely used today as a divinatory method and a system infused with esoteric symbolism. His book *The Doctrine and Ritual of High Magic* was divided into twenty-two chapters. Each chapter was dedicated to one of the twenty-two letters of the Hebrew alphabet and the cards of the Major Arcana. This leads us to the Tarot's connection with the ancient Kabbalah or Qabalah (Jewish mysticism) and then further along to Hermetic Kabbalah, a Western form of esoteric teaching, mysticism (becoming one with God or the Absolute), and the occult (hidden or knowledge of the hidden).

THE GOLDEN PATH

As it transpired, the chief translator of Éliphas Lévi was Arthur Edward Waite of the Rider-Waite Tarot (1909), possibly the most famous and widely used Tarot deck to this day, hand-drawn by artist Pamela Colman Smith and published by William Rider. Originally influenced by Lévi but often highly critical of him, Waite drew out greater connections to alchemy, astrology, magick, and Hermeticism. He was a member of the Hermetic Order of the Golden Dawn, founded in 1888 by Freemasons Dr. William Wynn Westcott, Dr. William Robert Woodman, and Samuel Liddell MacGregor Mathers. The "Golden Dawn" was the first of three orders, although all three are often collectively referred to as the Golden Dawn. The first order taught esoteric (specialised knowledge) philosophy based on the Hermetic Kabbalah, and personal development through study and awareness of the four classical elements. It also shared the basics of astrology, Tarot divination, and geomancy. The second or Inner Order, the Rosae Rubeae et Aureae Crucis, taught magic, including scrying, astral travel, and alchemy. The Third Order was that of the Secret Chiefs, who were said to be highly skilled and masterful. They supposedly directed the activities of the lower two orders by spirit communication with the chiefs of the second order. Importantly, the Golden Dawn was highly unusual for its day, admitting both men and women as members. Among its distinguished members was English occultist Aleister Crowley, who, after a falling out, went on to establish his own ceremonial magic group, the A'A' (Argenteum Astrum), and of course create his own Tarot deck, the Thoth Tarot, painted vibrantly and masterfully by Lady Frieda Harris under Crowley's strict instructions. The project spanned five years, 1938–43, and in fact it was published only in 1969, after the death of both Crowley and Lady Harris. The Thoth deck also drew symbolism from science and philosophy, aspects featured throughout the Starman Tarot.

RE-VISION

Years before Crowley, Waite had taken it upon himself to create a revision—RE-VISION—of the Tarot in accordance with the Hermetic and kabbalistic influences. The bold art and design created by Pamela Colman Smith, British artist, illustrator, writer, publisher, and occultist who was invited into the order of the Golden Dawn through her friendship with the Irish writer and occultist W. B. Yeats. It's interesting to note that two women artists have been central to the development and visual energy of modern Tarot.

Now we have the influence of Hermeticism, the introduction of God or the Intelligence of Life as a Cosmic Magician. Much was gleaned from the Hermetic writings by Marsilio Ficino, an Italian scholar and Catholic priest who was one of the most influential humanist philosophers (potential, and agency of human beings) of the early Italian Renaissance. He was an astrologer, a reviver of Neoplatonism, in touch with the major academics of his day. He was the first translator of Plato's complete

works into Latin. Neoplatonists believe that human perfection and happiness are attainable in this world, without awaiting an afterlife. Perfection and happiness are seen as synonymous and can be achieved through philosophical contemplation. Seen from a higher perspective, we all return to the One from which we emanated.

THREE TIMES MAGIC

Ficino traced teachings back to "Hermes Trismegistus" (three times majestic, three times magic—the trinity). Hermes Trismegistus appears as a fusion of the Greek god Hermes (Mercury to the Romans) and the Egyptian deity Thoth, embodying the transmission of celestial knowledge and writing. The teachings attributed to him formed the bedrock of Hermeticism, bridging the gap between Greek and Egyptian wisdom traditions. Hermes was so significant as an energetic archetype in the human consciousness that Carl Jung, Swiss pioneering psychotherapist, psychologist, and mythologist, and founder of analytical psychology, connected him to his entire process of self-actualisation, a process he called "Individuation." Jung and other prominent thinkers also linked this archetype to the phenomenon of synchronicity, when related or connected events occur together in time, with no clear cause or explanation.

It is with the entrance of Hermes Trismegistus into the consciousness of the Tarot that we track forward to arrive at the essence of the current and futuristic communication within the *Starman Tarot*. The Starman and Hermes Trismegistus are Messengers of LIGHT. In this, our journey through the history of Tarot arrives at the real alchemy that produces the gold of the Tarot we experience today.

The *Starman Tarot* offers the message, the possibility, that the Tarot, in this enhanced form—visually, symbolically, and energetically—is delivering and decoding the magical, encrypted knowledge, spiritual evolution, and creative vision—the energetic pattern of Hermes Trismegistus, in unison with other high-frequency entities. The *Starman Tarot* seeks to transmit the combination of Thoth and Hermes alongside the Earth-Magic shamans and shamankas that speak and resonate throughout the deck in an energetic pattern set forth through time, to be revealed in greater and greater clarity according to the turning of the age—the end of the age of Pisces and the beginning of Aquarius. This is the ultimate purpose and guiding light of the *Starman Tarot*.

When the need is greatest, the messengers will appear!

THE MESSAGE OF THE STARMAN

The *Starman Tarot* points to the greater understanding of the TRUTH OF LIGHT: to shine light on the TRUTH–THOTH–TAROT–TORUS FIELD. The truth is revealed through us gaining greater depth of understanding of reality and the ability to directly commune with Light or what appears as the world, our bodies, our minds and souls, ALL OF WHICH ARE LIGHT. The *Starman Tarot* is a calling to your creative spirit, a message of activation and liberation from all the fear and doubts that have stopped you living your deepest truth and passion. It is time to SHINE. This is the catalyst for you to deliver your unique expression!

God / the Intelligence is in fact MAGICK–LIGHT–the Original Magick. In the Tarot, the Magician, the Magus, the Alchemist—the Starman—stands at number one. Bowie sang this Aquarian catalyst into modern consciousness with the song "Starman." If we open our minds to be blown, we can imagine the lyrics heralding the coming of a great emissary such as Hermes Trismegistus in his Aquarian form, the Starman. He arrives bearing gifts. The sexually ambiguous, beautiful, star-dwelling super-being, emissary of light, a new form of consciousness, a wonder-filled form of life, that wishes to manifest into our humanity. The Starman archetype arrives to share astonishing knowledge and wisdom, to synthesise the greatest mysteries of the earth's ancient past with new forms of experience and manifestation; the unison of myth, magic, science, and living systems.

The light of the physical sun reveals the bodies of things.

The light of the psyche reveals the patterns of mind.

The psychic light reveals the hidden workings of things.

Truth is a form of light; when it shines, darkness is eliminated. Moreover, there is also a spiritual sun, and through its brilliance we finally gain the vision to see past our limited concepts of death; light can take on any form: physical, mind, and spirit. In its resonant radiance, we are set free from the "reductionist" context that seeks to break down and dissect the human experience into its constituent parts, thereby imprisoning us in a meaningless, mechanistic, and uncaring universe. The Starman is the catalyst, the conduit of sheer life force that blazes through your reality if you dare to boldly journey beyond our conditioned world of repetition, discord, and resignation. Appearing out of the dark womb of space, of "no thing," he ignites the alchemical flame, shedding light on those darker parts of ourselves, our fears, guilt, and trauma, so that they may be reconfigured, understood, and transformed. Bindings and restrictions are released, the unconscious drivers made conscious, and there is new freedom and flow in life. We move from the pain of not knowing, "Who am I?," to fully realising who we are, what our life and what this world are asking us to express . . . in each moment, over and over. Expanding our consciousness and building the muscles of trust in life as it streams through our minds and bodies.

Hermeticists were essentially engaged in a rebellion in consciousness. They took the pursuit of the mystical experience into their own hands and developed a way of thinking about life and the world that helped them communicate with and directly experience what they called "a more visionary reality." Now once again, we are being called forth to ignite a new rebellion of consciousness. To transition into this new way of seeing and being, we must seek guidance from a higher power, a higher authority of consciousness. We can allow ourselves to open to just how miraculous we are, just how beautiful this world is when we enter a deep, meaningful, and loving conversation with Nature and the Spiritual Light from which everything is manifest. Every element within the *Starman Tarot* is an invitation into that conversation.

The "Temple of God" is your body, an expression of light.

The journey of life is from the Fool, the Sacred Clown, to the World in the Major Arcana and then through all the suits of the Minor Arcana and back to the Sacred Clown, the Fool and the "beginner's mind." Arriving back at the Sacred Clown, having traversed the world and adventured with its many ancient archetypes, we can now rest inside the open question "Who Am I?" You see the cosmic joke; in fact, you were always perfectly at home. The *Starman Tarot* teaches the path to realization and salvation through healing and vitalising the physical body and seeing the mind's workings; knowing that we are an expression of the Great Intelligence of Light. In a world saturated with moving digital light, incessant noise and distractions, separation and the race against time, we appear to have lost the magical instruction manual for bringing awe, balance, and beauty to life. Creations such as the *Starman Tarot* arrive to correct that loss.

Your life is a work of art; the invitation here is for you to become the artist alchemist, the lover alchemist, the healer alchemist, the nature alchemist, the technology alchemist, the warrior alchemist, and on it goes, in service to something ASTONISHING. The *Starman Tarot* confirms that You are the Artist and the Art, the world is your canvas. As Terence McKenna so beautifully said, "The artist's task is to save the soul of mankind: anything less is a dithering while Rome burns. If the artist cannot find the way, then the way cannot be found."

And so, the evolution of Tarot unfolds, rich with the abundant unisons of teachings and mysteries to assist you in your journey through your life . . .

You come from the stars, and it is to the stars you will return.

THE WORKINGS OF A TAROT DECK

The Tarot is a system or map whose components reflect back to us the different parts of ourselves (our selves), acknowledging the tremendous trials and opportunities available. Each card is a shape-shifter able to convey multiple dimensions and offering different views and perspectives. It is organised into the Major Arcana of twenty-two cards (0–XXI): (0) THE SACRED CLOWN (fool), (I) THE STARMAN (magician, alchemist), (II) HIGH PRIESTESS, (III) THE EMPRESS, (IV) THE EMPEROR, (V) THE HIEROPHANT, (VI) THE LOVERS, (VII) THE CHARIOT, (VIII) STRENGTH, (IX) THE ALIEN (hermit), (X) THE WHEEL, (XI) JUSTICE, (XII) HANGED MAN, (XIII) DEATH, (XIV) TEMPERANCE, (XV) THE DEVIL, (XVI) THE TOWER, (XVII) THE STAR, (XVIII) THE MOON, (XIX) THE SUN, (XX) JUDGEMENT, (XXI) THE WORLD.

The Major Arcana convey universal principles and the fundamental operating systems of life. The big magic, the greater workings of reality. These are the things that act upon us, most often beyond our scope to control their will or directive. That said, some forces we can learn to master and manipulate or direct toward an objective. However, just as we cannot stop the snow in winter or the turning of the seasons, we must learn how to skilfully navigate these greater forces, coming into alignment, working with them, and seeing when we are shouting at the wind, so to speak.

The Minor Arcana consists of fifty-six cards, with four suits: PENTACLES, CUPS, SWORDS, and WANDS. Each suit has fourteen cards—ace through ten, plus four "court cards." This links to the kabbalistic philosophy of the four worlds: Atzilluth, the world of emanation (spirit); Beriah, the world of creation (thought); Yetzirah, the world of formation (emotion); and finally Assiyah, the world of action. The elements in order are fire, air, water, and earth, so the accepted order of the Tarot

suits is Wands, Swords, Cups, and Pentacles. The suits can be understood to refer to how we relate and move through our daily activities and relationships.

The court cards depict the archetypal nuclear family and their influence on the querent: KING, QUEEN, PRINCE, and PRINCESS. They reflect both the elemental quality ascribed to the suit and the personification of the masculine and feminine principles according to their maturity.

THE PRINCESS: Represents the youngest, with its youthful feminine power and exuberance, refreshing curiosity, and pristine potential, with much to learn, marking the ages of birth through to twenty-one in both genders. Playful, receptive, the one who will give birth to new perspectives, fresh facets of creativity plucked from reality, free and uncontaminated/unscathed by the trials and upsets of life. The Princesses are the quadrants of the astrological chart, often pregnant from/with the energy and elemental force that the ace of their suit carries. They embody the energy of a suit, rather than just their own representation.

THE PRINCE: Signifies young adulthood in both sexes, with the need to adventure, fiercely test, and explore the world, proving their ability. Unwilling to blindly accept what has been done before, the Prince is prone to rashness, impatience, and bravado, while at the same time having the sensitivity to reflect how the next generation carefully views what has gone before and becomes committed not to make the same mistakes.

THE QUEEN: The archetypal feminine, epitomises the visceral and spiritual nature of each of the elements guiding and shaping the interior life. Heart-based, this energy personified is relational, highly intuitive, and creative, the perfect powerful balancing force to the active and dynamic King. However, the feminine energy of the Queen can also be utterly formidable and passionately committed to life and what she believes in. She embodies the power of all the mothers through time, the countless births, the intimate suckling and nurturing, and a willingness to view life from many different perspectives.

THE KING: The archetypal masculine, expresses the masterful, directive, controlling, and authoritative quality of the suit, the great "doer" concerned with the tangible materiality of the world, accessible to male and female alike. The King embodies the power and protection of all fathers through time and must accept ultimate responsibility for both good and bad outcomes in the world. Not all Kings accept this gladly. He must give orders and at the same time be willing to take wise council, as did King Arthur by surrounding himself with multiskilled knights and the magical wisdom of Merlin.

While the Major Arcana Tarot card meanings reveal events that will naturally occur due to laws of the universe, the Minor Arcana Tarot card meanings reveal events that naturally occur due to laws of human nature. Therefore, the Minor Arcana highlight the more practical aspects of life and can refer to current issues that have a temporary or minor influence. The numbering of the ten cards reflects the qualities of each of the ten Sephiroth named in the Kabbalah, the Tree of Life of the Jewish mystic tradition that is seated at the centre of Western magick.

THE ELEMENTS AND TAROT

The elements have a highly significant influence, with each element imparting different qualities and relational aspects that you can use to enhance the communication of a card.

WANDS—FIRE: lighting, licking, scorching, brightening, blazing, heating, dancing, sizzling, sparking, crackling, smoking, smouldering, suffocating, flickering, flaming, lightening, roaring, roasting, burning, melting, warming, gleaming, glowing, igniting, kindling, radiating, catalysing, reacting, transforming

Energetic qualities, passion, courage, motivation, and drive to make something happen, to initiate. Behind many of our actions, the Wands suit is there to propel us forward, to move us to change something in our lives. The concept of energy is the capacity to do work or cause change. The law of conservation of energy states that it can neither be created nor destroyed; rather, it is converted from one form to another, in the process of transformation. Wands therefore represent energy, whether it's kinetic, thermal, electrical, chemical, nuclear, potential, or other forms, providing the power that ultimately drives our actions in the world. The heat and light of the sun make it possible for life to exist on Earth; captured by plants in photosynthesis, releasing oxygen and carbohydrates that power our bodies. Without the electromagnetic radiation that travels from the sun, the earth would simply freeze, with no winds, ocean currents, or clouds to transport water. Without our own energy source, we become lethargic, cold, and inactive. The fire of Wands then warms, moves, and expands, transmitting vitas to bodily cells and planetary systems so that we have the energy to create tangible things, to work. It stirs, activates, and galvanises human creativity, propelling exploration and innovations in the arts and sciences, with the potential to bring ever greater balance and beauty to life. Burning away what is no longer needed, it lights up the truth of events and circumstances—bringing tasks into clear sight. The torch that lights the way.

The magic of fire: Prometheus, one of the Titans in Greek mythology, defied the Olympian gods by taking fire from them and giving it to humanity, a technology that could be used to enhance civilization. He was severely punished and condemned to eternal torment by Zeus, king of the Olympian gods, by being bound to a rock and having his liver, which regenerated at night, be pecked out every day by an eagle. He stole fire from the workshop of Hephaestus, the god of fire, volcanoes, and blacksmithing, and patron of artisans and craftsmen, and passed it, hidden in a stalk of fennel, on to humankind. So the element of fire is very much linked to our human ability to artfully manifest thoughts and ideas.

CUPS—WATER: calming, clearing, cleansing, washing, ebbing, flowing, racing, gushing, crashing, stilling, burbling, foaming, frothing, overflowing, flooding, dampening, soaking, sparkling, rippling, trickling, showering, pouring, sprinkling, drowning, spilling, refreshing, dissolving, carrying, surrendering, shaping, filling, condensing, evaporating

Emotional qualities (e-motion—energy in motion), blood, the flow of liquids, the sacred feminine, the chalice, water from the stone—stone to water to wine. Water is

vital to our health and plays a key role in transporting nutrients, including oxygen within the blood, to the body's cells, while also carrying wastes to be eliminated. It is indeed nature's most remarkable solvent, allowing for all manners of substance to be moved through space and time. Enabling powerful methods of transport around the world, rivers and seas carried merchant traders, explorers, conquerors, and settlers. Natural waterways could be engineered to aid the fertility of the land and support a healthy ecology. When water is left to stand for long periods of time, it becomes stagnant; without the natural filtering of movement and aeration, water then becomes a breeding ground for harmful organisms. Similarly, emotions are currents of life force that react to external stimuli and run deep within the body, the deep waters of character, of beliefs about ourselves and the meaning of life. When these are denied, repressed, or ignored, they become stagnant and stuck. They're unable to be processed, witnessed, and attended to, so that they can move freely and be released from the body/mind system, and the resulting blockage creates emotional, behavioural, and physical symptoms. Developing and improving one's emotional intelligence, understanding and influencing emotional currents through techniques such as breathwork, and recognising them in those around you then helps bring about resourceful states of calmness, flow, and clarity, qualities that enhance leadership. Concurrently, cultural tides shape the overall context and environment in which we show up and are nurtured within. Water cleanses and washes away the dirt, makes things clean. Water makes things lush and juicy, but it can also destroy and wash away things that are valuable. The Cups that collect and hold the life-giving properties of water will sustain and nourish our well-being only if there is a state of flow, and like the water cycle of the earth itself, there is continuous movement. The Cups then invite us to keep moving on all levels to stay healthy and not stagnate. To endeavour to be in a state of flow, to know that a higher power moves the great river of existence.

The fourth phase of water: We have all learnt that water (H_2O) has three phases: solid, liquid, and gas, but recently Gerald H. Pollack, a professor of bioengineering, has uncovered a fourth phase, known as exclusion zone (EZ) water. This phase occurs next to water-loving (hydrophilic) surfaces and is found to exist almost everywhere in nature, including the human body, comprising 72–75 percent of water. Incidentally, the popular adage that we must drink at least 4 litres of water to stay hydrated is incorrect; not only have drinks such as skimmed milk and tea been found to be more hydrating, but we've overestimated our liquid requirements by up to a third. The fourth phase of water is liquid crystalline in composition—in other words, "structured," and there is evidence that the radiant energy of the sun, especially infrared energy, is what builds it. This discovery has profound implications for cell biology, especially how to impact cellular efficiency and noninvasive regenerative therapies.

PENTACLES—EARTH: fertilising, moistening, sinking, stilling, rooting, grounding, regenerating, nourishing, nurturing, decomposing, recycling, regenerating, clogging, solidifying, earthing, manifesting, structuring, building, gravitating, constructing, stabilising, conserving, weighting, crystallising, propagating, feeding, fortifying, sowing, seeding, forming

Physical qualities: structures of matter, the relationship of atoms made up of the elementary particles, quarks, and leptons. Matter takes up space and has a measurable

mass. Of the eight planets in our solar system, four are rocky and four are gas giants. Our planet Earth is the third planet from the sun and the only known astronomical object to support life, including our own, with the provision of shelter, food, and medicines. The earth's ecosystems are the communities of living and nonliving organisms that interact with each other and their environment, such as tropical and temperate forests, mangrove forests, tundra, grasslands, peat bogs, and agricultural land. Earth represents the mineral kingdom, which comprises over four thousand minerals, each with its own unique chemical makeup and crystalline structure that have evolved over the 4.5 billion years of Earth's history and generously support all life in the animal and vegetable kingdoms.

The physical plane connects us to the tangible forms in our lives that touch, nurture, support, protect, and nourish us. Four elements—carbon, hydrogen, nitrogen, and oxygen—are essential to every living thing and collectively make up 99 percent of the mass of protoplasm, with phosphorus and sulfur being essential to the structure of nucleic acids and amino acids, respectively. The remaining essential elements for life and their patterns in the physical body are calcium, chlorine, magnesium, potassium, and sodium, key to membrane activity and osmosis, and, finally, carbon, so present throughout the body. The second-most-common element in the body, making up about 18 percent of body mass after oxygen (66 percent, predominantly in water), it is found in many bonded compounds that make up bones, muscles, organs, and our skin, nails, and hair. Astonishingly, 98 percent of the atoms in the human body are renewed each year, so many of the nearly thirty trillion human cells are replaced regularly, with the *average* age of all cells in the human body being seven to ten years, while some cells, such as those in the colon, are replaced every three to five days, and others, such as our fat and muscle cells, take up to seventy years to renew.

The remarkable structures inanimate and animate that populate our world of form, of defined mass, inherently point to nature's resources and cycles, of composition and decomposition. The suit of Pentacles also refers to objects and technologies invented and made by the human hand to assist us in life; everything from harvesting cotton for clothing, to the use of natural resources such as crude oil, coal, cellulose, salt, and natural gas to make the miracle of plastic. The Pentacles also represent the huge diversity of technologies that we use to thrive in the material world, such as money. It is what we build, what's lasting, and what is necessary. The Great Mother Earth, the home of us all and the earth to which we must all eventually return.

SWORDS—AIR: flowing, flying, breathing, blowing, puffing, purifying, humidifying, drying, refreshing, swaying, blasting, wafting, playing, travelling, transporting, circulating, ventilating, polluting, moistening, warming, swirling, speeding, whirling, permeating, cleansing, calming, revitalising, clarifying, carrying.

Mental qualities: intellect—thought—the power of thinking. Cognition is the mental process of acquiring knowledge and understanding through thought, experience, and the senses. Breath is the bridge that connects life to consciousness, which unites your body to your thoughts. Just as a sharp sword can cut through obstacles, intellect has the ability to cut through ignorance, confusion, and falsehood, leading to clarity and insight. The mind cuts incoming information from the senses into pieces, breaks things down into their component parts, and analyses them, contrasting and comparing,

evaluating and synthesising, to arrive at a conclusion. When individuals don't cultivate and use their intellect, they may fall prey to superstitions, false beliefs, and misguided ideologies. They become vulnerable to manipulation and exploitation. To be in relationship with the world and others through the mind—the mental activity—we are encouraged to develop the faculty of critical thinking. Words are swords that can cut through confusion, emotion, and wishful thinking and cut open ideas to see the quintessence of things. They can also create tremendous internal and outer conflict, misunderstanding, pain, and regret. This is the realm of communication: music, linguistics, the sciences and mathematics, learning, acquiring knowledge and making inferences, presupposing, and contextualising, drawing out the distinctions that lead to understanding. Air is that marvellous conductor of sound enabling us to speak, express, listen, and understand one another and so live and develop cooperative societies.

The atmosphere, a layer of gas and suspended solids, surrounds the earth and holds the air we breathe, protecting us from outer space and holding moisture (clouds), gases, and tiny particles. Nitrogen is the most prevalent of the gases, diluting oxygen and preventing rapid burning at the earth's surface. Of all the elements, air is probably the element that we take for granted the most. Ever present, invisible, so intrinsic to our lives that we don't give it a second's thought until we experience a lack of breath. We never fully appreciate it until we are suddenly deprived of it. Just as we ceaselessly breathe, so do we ceaselessly think, communicate, and relate to the world. Your mind is the space between your current consciousness and higher consciousness, and air is the great intermediary, circulating, filling, the space in between.

ASTROLOGY AND THE TAROT

For many, the Tarot can also be viewed in terms of astrology and the signs of the zodiac. For our purpose here in demonstrating the relationship, we will simply reference the Major Arcana, where each of the cards is associated with a sign of the zodiac, a planet, or element. Consequently, it is divided as follows: 12-7-3. Much of this will intuitively make sense. Feel free to check out www.davidedeangelis.com to discover more about this subject.

12

♈ ARIES: The Emperor—Fire
♉ TAURUS: The Hierophant—Earth
♊ GEMINI: The Lovers—Air
♋ CANCER: The Chariot—Water
♌ LEO: Strength—Fire
♍ VIRGO: The Alien (hermit)—Earth
♎ LIBRA: Justice—Air
♏ SCORPIO: Death—Water
♐ SAGITTARIUS: Temperance—Fire
♑ CAPRICORN: The Devil—Earth
♒ AQUARIUS: The Star—Air
♓ PISCES: The Moon—Water

7

☿ MERCURY: The Starman (magician)—Air
♀ VENUS: The Empress—Earth
☾ MOON: High Priestess—Water
♃ JUPITER: The Wheel—Fire
♂ MARS: The Tower—Fire
☉ SUN: The Sun—Fire
♄ SATURN: The World—Earth

3

🜁 AIR: The Sacred Clown (fool)
🜄 WATER: The Hanged Man
🜂 FIRE: Judgement

TAROT AND THE HUMAN BODY

One final aspect we'd like to briefly touch upon is the powerful relationship between the Tarot and the human body—an area often overlooked or dismissed. These associations vary across different schools of thought, and there's no single "correct" way to interpret them. As you work more intimately with the cards, you'll find your own intuitive connections emerging.

Exploring the body through the lens of Tarot can offer profound insights, especially when navigating persistent physical issues and their links to thought patterns, emotional states, and energetic imbalances. Toxic beliefs, relationships, environmental pollutants, and dietary toxins can all impact the body—often manifesting within one or more of it's twelve core systems: integumentary (skin, hair, nails), skeletal, muscular, nervous, endocrine, circulatory, lymphatic, immune, respiratory, digestive, urinary, and reproductive.

Each system can be seen as an archetypal landscape, rich with meaning and potential for healing. For example, the nervous system might resonate with The Starman, symbolizing consciousness, electrical intelligence, and dynamic awareness. The circulatory system may align with The Lovers or The Empress, reflecting the flow of love, nourishment, and connection.

Meditating on the Tarot in relation to your body can unlock a multidimensional understanding of your physical, emotional, and spiritual well-being. It invites you into a deeper dialogue with your internal landscape, helping you restore harmony, access transformative wisdom, and engage in meaningful self-healing.

In the image below, notice how The Chariot can be mapped onto different brain functions and physical structures—highlighting the Tarot's capacity to mirror our biological complexity.

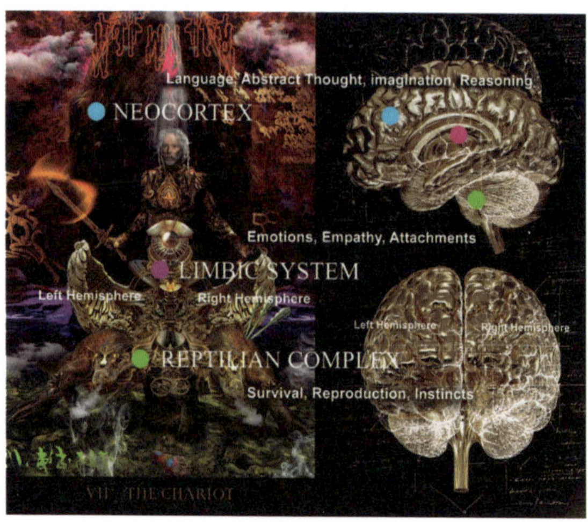

HOW TO USE THE TAROT

It will serve you to create an uncluttered, calm, and supportive environment and atmosphere when giving yourself or anyone else a reading, facilitating a clear approach and intention. Invite your intuition, the feeling sense in your body, to be present and help it ask, guide, and interpret the cards. As with any form of "journeying," it is beneficial to focus your energy, deciding perhaps which area of your life is the most deserving of your attention. From your perspective, what one thing would make the biggest difference to your life right now? And if you didn't change this, what will it cost you in the short and the long run? Is it still a major game changer? If so, asking the Tarot for greater insight, clarity, and perspective may be very beautiful. The major dramatic themes of life—love, birth, death, destiny, and prosperity—all shine their light into the question of "What is it that you really want?" What seeds need to be planted, where, and how? What dreams are being lit?

THE STARMAN SPREAD

TO ILLUMINATE YOUR RADIANT POTENTIAL

The Star, like our sun, is a dazzling emissary, guiding and illuminating a pathway through the great mystery of space and time. The ancient symbol of the Pythagoreans, so emblazoned on flags around the world, is a vivid representation of harmonic brilliance and unity. Use the Starman Spread to unify and catalyse the brilliance you wish to create in your work and relationships, allowing the Divine Radiance to shine forth and light up new personas and possibilities.

CARD 1: The energy source that carries the greatest potential for illumination at this time.

CARD 2: Your female ancestors—the part of the feminine that needs to be acknowledged and expressed.

CARD 3: Your male ancestors—the part of the masculine that needs to be experienced and made manifest.

CARD 4: What is most holding you back and needs to be healed and integrated at this time?

CARD 5: What energy trait will assist you and carry you purposefully forward?

CARD 6: What you are growing into—your radiance and shining potential.

THE LIGHTNING BOLT SPREAD

TO CATALYSE A CREATIVE PROJECT

Lightning is a complex, multistage process: a symbol of light striking through ignorance—the bolt of electric magic that conducts energy from space to Earth. It epitomizes the epiphany, an awakening to something stunning and new, channeling an entirely fresh array of colours and meanings within the spectrum of your reality. Use the Lightning Bolt Spread to ignite a new project or phase in your life. Allow it to show you the unexpected and spark a new exterior and interior territory.

CARD 1: The seed—the lightning catalyst, the spark that ignites and sets the project and life force in motion.

CARD 2: The vision expressed—the new possibility in service to the world in authentically declared—the creative vehicle for the potent message.

CARD 3: The heart—the strike of love that awakens the deep healing potential and connection that is possible through this process.

CARD 4: The powerful urge—the energy, devotion, and enthusiasm required to harness resources and propel the project forward.

CARD 5: The ultimate manifestation—the unique essence, energy, and specific form that heralds its birth into the world.

THE MAJOR ARCANA

0 / THE SACRED CLOWN (THE FOOL):
I LAUGH AT THE GAME OF LIFE.

The Sacred Clown, or Heyoka from the Lakota tradition, knows that nothing we think is ultimately true; no belief is fixed. As trickster and shaman converge, he probes beneath the veil of normality to reveal the astonishing and unexpected, indeed the gap between you and what you have understood to be you. His words are like a lightning bolt that can pierce the heart. This card depicts the Sacred Clown, dressed in a black-and-white-striped antler hat, grinning mischievously as a burst of flames shoots from his finger. Bare chested, painted to the waist, he is surrounded by walls of garish graffiti that appear to be alive, morphing, moving strands of hypnotic colour bursting with energy. Standing on a path bedecked with sharp-toothed traps of ill-gotten gold, he appears utterly unconcerned that they could cause him injury. An almighty star ball of molten fire glows and puckers close behind, and he is indifferent. He is touched by everything and damaged by nothing, seeing the cosmic joke, the ultimate illusion, where we see limitation, fear, and pain. At once both innocent and dangerous, his fire pokes holes in the things you take too seriously. He incinerates the fabric of your stories, the triumphs and woes of the past, the projected fears of the future, because

he understands that the primordial energy of nature is beyond good and evil, beyond human ideas of right and wrong. Joy and pain are united, two sides of the same coin. For me, no other character so epitomised Bowie as the Heyoka, the rapier-sharp, wise innocent, the Sacred Clown. Bowie was an absolute master at piercing reality to expose the absurd. He was never afraid to experiment and discard the design brief when something perverse and unexpected caught our attention. The enlightened player of the game of life, the contrarian, the challenger of convention. When working together, we celebrated the risk, dancing on the creative edge. Often, his visits to our studio would result in howls of laughter, such as the time I smuggled a full-sized "replica" of a bull's head into the studio, under the cover of darkness to avoid a media frenzy, and the outrage (rightly so) from animal rights advocates. Waiting in the wings, they were under the false impression that Bowie had sacrificially killed a bull for the "Outside" photo shoot. That provocative spirit of the Sacred Clown travels through each card of the *Starman Tarot*, twisting things around and turning them on their head. Christ the sacred clown mocked orthodoxy, Buddha the sacred clown mocked ego attachment, while Gandhi mocked money and power. He invites you to risk, to risk big—that you must risk the sting and bite of life to experience its true wonder and opportunity. This card invites you to live in the exciting potential and freedom of each moment. The Heyoka provokes, prods, and startles you out of the hypnotic trance of the monkey mind. He bids you be aware that you are not the stream of fear and desire endlessly surfacing, but rather the expansive freedom in which these issues appear and disappear. When you say "I . . . ," you are referring to your story. Your story is not true. The burdens that you have carried for so long can be put down because they never belonged to you. Feel into your body, be flexible. Something new awaits you on unexplored paths, so step into life fearlessly. Renew, refresh, and rebirth yourself—you are a star child; feel the inner laughter.

Reversed: Feeling trapped by the burden of responsibilities and the goad of past regrets. There is a danger of acting rashly with little regard to other people's well-being. While it is appropriate to follow the heart and a true calling, it is immature to run away from one's obligations. Unfinished business will follow you around and diminish your life potential, so take stock despite any impatience and longing for freedom. The power to act rather than react. Settle your accounts, heal your relationships, and don't act until you are clearer of resentments and false beliefs.

Summary

The Sacred Clown:

Piercing reality to expose the absurd. The stories you tell yourself about who you are and what's possible in life aren't true; renew and refresh and rebirth yourself—you are a child, innocent and free. **Reversed:** Feeling trapped by the burden of responsibilities. Have patience, take stock, and renegotiate your obligations before you follow your heart and true calling.

I / THE STARMAN (THE MAGICIAN): I WILL BLOW YOUR MIND.

The Starman is an attractor field through which we can observe the self we believe to be true. We are being invited to see the inherent nature of the human condition and look at what has been fashioned by culture through the ages; the belief and value systems we have simply adopted. His glorious presence awakens us to see another realm entirely, and in that resonance, seemingly irrefutable facts are seen as fictions. We see the Starman, Aquarian catalyst bringing the seed of transformation to the world, carrying the double helix, the source of our ancestry, in one hand, and the golden key that unlocks our supreme potential in the other hand. The unison of myth, magic, science, and living systems. The Luminous One descending to Earth with his arms outstretched, the alien messiah, a beautiful, star-dwelling emissary. A vision of ecstatic colour, light, and fire, molecular worlds streaming tendrils of life-giving substance. Travelling through space, surrendered in time, ripples in the exosphere, his presence shimmering with ancient symmetries, waiting for the moment to reveal his power . . . because he knows it will blow our minds. Like the Greek god Hermes, he can travel freely between different realms, between the mortal and divine worlds, dreams, and waking states. The Starman releases a palpable sense of creative potency in the air—a hidden potential demanding to be realised. The dissolving of the Starman's

solid form into the golden pool of liquid light, his sheer willingness to melt himself down to be reborn as something fresh, something new, but that which still contains all the elements woven from the past, is a powerful metaphor. We too can place the personality and the various jaded facets of ourselves into the flame of the creative fire to be reconfigured in ever-more-liberating expressive and complex ways. We must throw ourselves into the white-hot flames and, despite this heat and sheer intensity, know that we can never disappear. To boldly confront the fear of destroying that which we cherish, something complete and comfortable, with great intrinsic value, and yet be courageous and break it down. To trust the Starman as he propels us toward the possibility of discovering what we didn't know that we didn't know—revealing the raw components of life, with all the thoughts, frailties, passions, and anxieties that can now be transformed and recombined into something powerful, impactful—extraordinary. He knows that power does not come from him, but through him, and he wields it with absolute integrity, creating something magical out of nothing. The Starman offers us the elixir—a constant visual theme (and quest) in my work with Bowie. How to create images that brought things to the surface to be seen, felt, and, ultimately, to be healed of its own destruction. We must risk our own destruction, risk our own failure, and embrace what appears to be a mistake. Bowie seized upon things that would have been viewed as insignificant, and these were often the things that bore the most fruit. He wasn't afraid to pull things apart that already looked finished, to reveal something unexpected and significant. When the Starman appears, it is a signal to see what elements of your life can be reinvented and rethought in order to create and reveal something extraordinary. He is calling you to discover your full creative potential.

No Reverse for this card.

SUMMARY

THE STARMAN:

A hidden potential demanding to be realised. A signal to see what elements of your life can be reinvented and rethought in order to create and reveal something extraordinary—living alchemy. Reconfigure yourself in liberating, expressive, and beautifully complex ways. Turn your life into a compelling work of art.

II / THE HIGH PRIESTESS:
I OFFER UP THE MYSTERIES OF LIFE.

The High Priestess is the guardian of the mysterious, subtle, and deeper aspects of life that are not visible or obvious. She has command of the esoteric knowledge and sacred wisdoms that are part of the collective unconscious—that which we are unaware of even existing. Associated with the moon and the wellspring of life and movement lurking in the deep, dark waters, she embodies deepest innate wisdom, the knowledge and wisdom of Mother Nature, of healing, "la medicina." As the keeper of your unconscious, she sits at the liminal boundary between what you are aware of and the vast spectrum of the unseen inner realms. Traditionally conceived as the passive, receptive feminine calmly waiting for life to unfold, she manifested for me as this powerful force of nature that journeys between the visible and the invisible, part diva, part shamanka (shaman). Her clothes are adorned with snakes, which from a Celtic perspective are symbolic of secret knowledge, cunning, and transformation, and points to the High Priestess's shape-shifting energy and utilisation of energy that is unseen. She is pictured crouching, streaks of lightning shooting from her fingertips as if to emphasise the two pillars B (Boaz—completion) and J (Jachin—begin) from Solomon's (soul of man) Temple in Jerusalem, formed as abstract typography with both meanings woven together. Her language is similarly abstract and often vague, with many symbolic

and metaphoric references requiring patience to decode. She signals the need to journey within, paying attention to your dreams and visions, sensing their relevance while acknowledging the synchronicities of the symbols and events that appear in your physical world. Listen to the powerful stirrings of your intuition, your gut feelings—you already possess the most powerful guidance system in the entire universe. The High Priestess, therefore, invites you to be still, to meditate, to explore the mystery of life, witnessing the mind and becoming more aware of your feeling nature. As the feminine receptive principle, she perfectly balances the masculine desire to shape and master the physical world by calling us to reflect deeply on that which actively stirs our hearts. The High Priestess, otherworldly and sensual, with a whole-body intelligence, indicates this shift in context, the providence of embodying a vastly new way of "being" that, when combined with the masculine active worldly principle of the Magician, can release immense power, knowledge, and goodness into the world. Out of the soil that was your old life, your old way of being, believing and reacting to the world, a new form and its expression can germinate. Choose that this is a benevolent reality, a kind universe, and let the seeds of your potential naturally blossom.

Reversed: The shadow of the High Priestess casts seeds of doubt and mistrust into your thoughts and deeds. Ignoring the call to transform, you will fall back into the sleep of bland conformity. The issues and painful beliefs, that stuck energy lodged deep in your cellular structure, will continue to grow unchecked, eating away, aging rather than rejuvenating you. Don't let the past define and dictate what you know about yourself and life; instead, uncover fresh ways of exploring life; otherwise, distracting, denying, and possibly dangerous addictive habits can surface, dimming your radiant potential.

SUMMARY

THE HIGH PRIESTESS:

The wellspring of life, the deep waters of the unconscious, innate wisdom, and magick of Mother Nature. Signalling the need to journey within, paying attention to dreams and visions. Choose that this is a benevolent reality, a kind universe, and let the seeds of your potential naturally grow. **Reversed:** Painful beliefs, stuck energy lodged deep in your cellular structure, will continue to grow unchecked unless you are willing to forgive and discover fresh, life-affirming ways of exploring life.

III / THE EMPRESS:
I FULLY EMBRACE LIFE'S RICH FECUNDITY.

As the archetypal Mother, the Empress embodies Mother Nature and the various seasons of life from birth through to death. She understands that to fully embrace life, we must experience its remarkable hues; ready and open to accept the joy, love, and happiness, together with the pain, loss, and sadness. What is born will eventually die, and thus we must enjoy, relax, and open to each day we have, understanding the cycles of birth, death, and rebirth. She is the embodiment of summer—ripe, bursting with vitality, creativity, abundance, and prosperity—a conduit for powerful sensual pleasure, beauty, and sexuality; fecundity that is heartily celebrated by her. The milk of life pours from her breasts, and indeed she has the milk of kindness in her, knowing how to attend to creation, nurturing and full of warmth, love, generosity, and patience. She is created here as a beautiful blend of Caucasian, Asian, and African heritage, the Mother of the World, her presence weaving a potent gateway for all. Seated on a megalithic stone similar to that at Newgrange, the Passage Grave, built in Ireland around 3200 BCE and embellished with perhaps one of the oldest symbols of human spirituality, the spiral, she is mistress of her womb-like domain. The ancients lived by a womb cosmology of creation, in which everything was birthed and dissolved through a womb space, in waves of cosmic cycles. As every being is birthed through a womb, so scientists

believe that the universe was birthed by a giant black hole, a cosmic womb. The spiral that is so prominent in plants and natural systems, such as the weather and our own galaxy, the Milky Way, and was such an important symbol for the Celts is presumed to mean the balance of inner and outer consciousness—we will never know because the Druids of Celtic polytheism (paganism) were forbidden to ever write about sacred material. A gilded bird's cage floats above the Empress's head, with a tiny bird flying free, suggesting that despite appearances, the door to freedom is always open—we can all be free as a bird. She invites us to abandon oneself to her and let her mysterious energy infuse your creations, fuelling the birth of eventual form or structure. The world would certainly be out of balance, and therefore ugly, if everyone was a painter, singer, or dancer; nevertheless the spirit of creativity is nourishing to all. When your creativity so totally infuses your life, every moment is seen living with creative potential; you live in God. This card also invites you to nourish and nurture your own vehicle of transformation, your body—that which was given by the miracle of Nature despite the imperfections you see. Attend to the balance and beauty of your physical environment, especially your home and the natural world around you.

Reversed: The abundance and ease that the upright Empress delivered has evaporated as you sink into murky muddy challenges . . . the more you resist, the deeper in you get. You must find healthful ways to replenish yourself and connect to your own natural source of creativity and personal development. A needy mother or maternal figure may be depleting your own energy sources, so establishing personal boundaries is vital. This phase too shall pass.

SUMMARY

THE EMPRESS:

Fecundity—ripe, bursting with vitality, creativity, abundance, and sensual pleasure. Nurture and discover the miracle of Nature that is your own body; relax and open to the joy available each day and bring beauty to your environment. **Reversed:** Lack of vitality, ignoring the creative sensual side of your nature. Establish healthful boundaries and seek out healthful ways to replenish yourself and your source of creativity.

IV / THE EMPEROR:
I LEAD BY EXAMPLE.

The Emperor is the Paternal Father who instructs about the matters of responsibility, order, control, and discipline. He is a formidable character, a stern authority of the law, rules, and regulations that govern society. A man of great integrity, intellect, and strength, he assumes leadership, providing stability, security, and protection. He is a firm disciplinarian, and we do not always welcome our dealings with him, and yet, his righteousness, harshness, and punishment are enforced so that we can learn to be more self-disciplined and think logically and rationally rather than succumb to the rampant ride of emotion. Conceived by me as a fantastical space emperor donning his robes with theatrical flourish like some superhero from the genre of '80s sci-fi films, *Flash Gordon* and *Dune*, he is a contrived vision of both Abraham Lincoln and David Bowie. The neutron patterns centred at his navel, the power centre, symbolise knowledge combined with physical power. His palace is the brick-and-mortar extension of his mind, the architectural environment that fosters such intelligence. His world appears cold, with a fierce beauty deserving of healthy fear and respect. Not afraid of dealing with the harsh or grim realities and vicissitudes of life, he is able to make difficult decisions without enthusiastic or popular support. Practical and careful consideration is always employed with all the facts laid square, for he is keen to get to the real truth

and demands honesty. In complete contrast to the Empress, the Emperor rules with his head and not his heart and consequently does not suffer fools gladly. He has an iron will and a steel fist and is not afraid to wield both and therefore is suited to the courts of law, government, and the army, prepared to fight the good cause. To his left sits a pile of books containing the objective analysis and effective solutions that address the public and private sectors in his kingdom. To his right is a sextant, a remarkable instrument created almost three hundred years ago that measures the distance between astronomical objects and the horizon as he seeks to navigate his realm through space. His is an expression of hard-won victory and success, demanding determination and resilience. This card suggests you no longer have to prove yourself; your expertise and experience are unquestioned—it is time to lead by example. Get your house in order and regain control of an important area of your life so that you can live on your own terms, having the courage to walk your talk. It may be time to step up and approach your own father or father figure to pragmatically face and resolve a specific problem that is draining you and your life of vitality.

Reversed: There is a reluctance to take responsibility for your own situation or life circumstances, and excuses abound. It takes tremendous self-discipline and honesty, time, commitment, and a methodical approach to weigh up your priorities, make decisions, and plan for success, but it's necessary. Professional advice or coaching may be warranted.

SUMMARY

THE EMPEROR:

The formidable authority of law, order, and discipline, dealing with the practical and sometimes grim realities and vicissitudes of life. It's time to use your experience and expertise and lead by example. You are being called to take responsibility and have the courage to walk your talk. **Reversed:** Reluctance to be accountable for your life situation. Apply self-discipline and honesty to methodically approach your priorities, make decisions, and plan for success.

V / THE HIEROPHANT:

I AM THE TEACHER OF UNIVERSAL LAW.

The Hierophant is the guardian and custodian of religious knowledge and spiritual beliefs, a religious figure or guru (teacher), preserving and passing on knowledge intact. The masterful conduit of spiritual energy, he is admired and acknowledged as the teacher of God's Law, the keeper of spiritual wisdom passed down through millennia. He alone has access to this knowledge and, as the spiritual authority, is master of ceremonies, choosing wisely who is initiated into the ways of Spirit and Spiritual Governance. I have depicted the Hierophant as part man, part wolf. Probably the most misunderstood of all wild animals, wolves are seen merely as killing machines that hunt in packs—a scourge to be rid of—so much so that now, most species are considered endangered. Wolves in fact are extremely gregarious, mate for life, have strong family bonds and a clear clan structure, and deflect conflict where possible. Though their clans are highly organised, they are truly free spirits. A symbol of the night seen howling at the moon, they represent the lonely path of journeying within to learn and discover our inner power and strength. The wolf nature, though, also expresses the idiom of biblical origin used to describe the deceptiveness of appearance, a kind nature masking danger, the wolf in sheep's clothing. After all, religion has been a double-edged sword: a source for conflict and a resource for peace. Religion has been at the

heart of most violent conflicts, especially in the past two decades, and is worn as a badge of identity fuelling or abating conflict for political ends. The Hierophant, the channeller of male spiritual energy, can indeed bare his teeth. The flower of life, a flowerlike pattern with six-fold symmetry like a hexagon, floats above his head. This sacred geometry depicting the creation of existence, containing all the essential building blocks of the universe, which we call the Platonic solids, is found all over the world, in most religions and various ancient civilizations. It can be seen in temples within the Forbidden City of China, in ancient synagogues in Israel, in the Buddhist temples of India and Japan, while the oldest known examples are believed to be those present in the Temple of Osiris in Abydos, Egypt. Temples that have born witness to the visceral rituals and ceremonies of sacred sound and sight, scented aromas, and touch and taste, which have been used to reinforce the stories, doctrines, and values of religion. To serve God, one is actively encouraged either to live and pray in an enclosed spiritual community or to live in the secular world. Choosing then to pray/meditate and meet regularly in the House of God establishes a strong social structure and the idea of "belonging" and "contributing" to a bigger group or tribe. The Hierophant card calls you to investigate the existing sets of beliefs and systems that are already in place within your environment, and to see if they hold anything of value for you.

Reversed: You may be feeling constricted, suffocated by rules and convention, confined by "his story." There might be a need to throw off the shackles of the past and be a stand for something fresh and new. Explore other religious and spiritual beliefs and practices from around the world, especially those that are modern. It could be the perfect time to engage with "her story" and the stories and culture of Indigenous people to create and establish your own visceral rituals for transformation.

SUMMARY

THE HIEROPHANT:

Keeping spiritual wisdom and traditions intact. Investigate existing sets of beliefs and systems that surround you and bring the power of ritual to life. **Reversed:** Feeling constricted by convention and rules, confined by "his-story." Throw off the shackles of the past and be a stand for something fresh and new.

VI / THE LOVERS:
I AM THE GATEWAY TO DIVINE LOVE.

The Lovers govern the realm of relationships and relationship with self or another and ask us to consider different points of view so that we can "relate" to the issues at hand. Rather than see things as black *or* white, it encourages us to expand our point of view and see things as black *and* white, two sides of the same coin. The Lovers are depicted in an urban landscape, illustrating that most of our lives are now being played out in urban environments—we have moved out of the garden and into the city. Cities are gateways to new opportunities and experiences, diverse melting pots of culture, service, and learning. Similarly, the gateway of the Lovers archetype can expand our point of view, experiencing how different or "disowned" qualities complement and contribute to a greater and more potent sense of "being" and "possibility" in the world. We feel the magic of synergy; the whole being greater than the sum of its parts. The Lovers' faces are taken directly from a work of art I created for Bowie in 1997 also called *The Lovers*. Their nudity symbolises their desire to be open and free, honest, soulful, and sensual beings that feel safe, honoured, and appreciated in each other's presence . . . open to revealing their shadow selves and receiving the light of awareness and acceptance. Experiencing the "highs" of love and the associated high levels of dopamine in the brain, we can effortlessly fall in love with the self; our beauty, innocence,

and radiance reflected beautifully back to us by the other. We move with and beyond the ecstatic embraces, passionate, sensual, and embodied to merge and become one another, whole, complete. The bees dance above the honeycomb dripping with honey, the sensual and sweet food of the gods, the ancient symbol of love and fertility believed to be a powerful aphrodisiac and incorporated into many ritual practices associated with fertility and marriage. The spider, a remarkable figure of feminine energy and creativity whose skill in weaving her intricate web is a miracle of organic engineering, symbolises weaving the web of life with her lover and the integration of all parts, light and dark, into a whole, while the bullet holes are a stark reminder of the destructive power of love, the addiction to a lover. Inherent in the art of relationship is two-way communication, giving and receiving, expressing, and listening, and when we realise that there are fuller gifts to give and receive beyond the passion of sexual love, love can then be transformed. From the heat of desire for the other, to a beautiful sharing and acknowledgment of the gift of life embodied and mirrored in each other. As the depth of loving grows and matures, the acceptance of "what will be will be," moment to moment, expands, and, like the fountain of life in an overflowing cup, each gives for the sheer joy of giving, wanting nothing in return. This card hums with positivity, balance, and harmony.

Reversed: Communication somewhere in your life is problematic, with a consequent breakdown of trust. Perhaps you have lost sight of what moves you to contribute to and sustain a significant relationship. Forgoing opportunities to clearly express your appreciation, spending high-quality time, and withholding your dreams and desires for the future is clearly damaging to both. The spiritual and sexual connection seems to be lost. It may be valuable to investigate and embody each other's primary "love language," thus guiding your relationship to health; see Gary Chapman's *The Five Love Languages*.

SUMMARY

THE LOVERS:

The art of communication, balance of giving and receiving, expanding awareness, and acceptance of difference. Feel the magick of synergy, blending opposing realities into one. Your cup is overflowing with the sheer joy of giving. **Reversed:** Communication breakdown; withholding appreciation, your dreams, and your desires for the future. Open to how different or disowned qualities complement and contribute to a more potent sense of "being."

VII / THE CHARIOT:

I AM CONFIDENT THAT WITH DISCIPLINE I WILL SUCCEED.

The Chariot is the war vehicle that carries this dreadlocked, life-wise king forward to victory against his enemies. His battle dress, demeanour, and maturity suggest that he has been navigating the battlefield for many years. In life, like Homer's great champion and Trojan War hero, Odysseus, who in the *Odyssey* faces tremendous travails on his long return home after the war, the ingenious early-won victories turn to absurdly challenging battles requiring enormous tenacity. Weathered by time, experience, and adversity, he knows that he will not be successful without rigorous preparation, planning, creativity, and, above all, self-control. He understands that he must rein in his emotions and control his natural aggression and ferocity while focusing his mind on what he wants to achieve. He must not get carried away by his ambition and imagination. Balancing head with heart, masculine with feminine, he knows he must travel with complete concentration and awareness on the difficult path, all the while keeping his wheels in motion. Without control, the Komodo dragons pulling his great chariot will run wild and make a bid for freedom. The Chariot itself is part organic tree and part mechanism, expressing the means by which humanity has sought to engineer and collaborate with nature. The venomous Komodo dragons, which we had the privilege of seeing firsthand on the island of Gili Meno in Indonesia, are powerful

predators, capable of taking down large prey with their great serrated teeth. They appear slow and cumbersome, but these lizards are all muscle and can move at explosive speed, a powerful reminder to trust our own survival instincts. The card therefore implies that the game of life can be won only if we can master our emotions, controlling our worries and fears, regrets, resignation, and hopelessness. The king driving his chariot symbolises that self-belief and confidence comes from consistently refocusing one's thoughts and ideas to the objective and goal at hand. We must move past the limbic system, the stress response of fight or flight, to engage with greater emotional intelligence. When we know ourselves, our motivations, and our needs—the *why* we do things, we can become more aware of when we are off track. The Chariot ultimately signifies hard-won success, and whatever this card is connected to demands completion. Finish what you start and, if you are working with people, maintain balance and harmony by acknowledging and affirming people's needs and feelings, while maintaining control. We can consciously and creatively release frustrations and engage in the power of positive self-talk, the mantra that will keep our wheels turning in the right direction. Although you must take people's needs and feelings into consideration, ultimately you must take full responsibility for your words and deeds. In this act sits the power to live on purpose.

Reversed: A situation is out of balance, and your emotions are running high with emotional outbursts that take you over. It indicates that your best path might be to retreat and focus on practices that reconnect you to inner stillness and calm, and, from that place, decide what you wish to let go of. Using the power of meditation, of seeing the flow of thoughts and self-talk as a stream of consciousness, noise even, rather than perceived reality or "the truth," we can give ourselves space to breathe new life force into our desires. Be prepared to ask for love and support from family, friends, and your higher self.

SUMMARY

THE CHARIOT:

The balance of head with heart, mastering emotions—fears, worries, and regrets. Masterminding a plan for success. You are being called to methodically finish what you have started; keep moving forward. **Reversed:** Out of balance and overwhelmed, retreat and regroup. Reconnect to inner stillness, purpose, and calm, using the power of meditation, space to breath new life force into your ambitions.

VIII / STRENGTH:

I FACE MY FEARS WITH THE STRENGTH OF LOVE AND PATIENCE.

While this card symbolises strength, its nature is very different and in great contrast to the masculine counterpart of strength, the Chariot. Sheer determination and will are not wielded; instead, the lions that symbolise our innate power and instincts, the frenzy and passion of our emotions, are tamed by the calm, loving, and sure touch of the feminine and purity of heart. The lions have deferred to her inner strength and self-mastery and know that they will not be harmed. She speaks the language of the heart and is fearless in its truth. The mandalas alive in the background behind her are generated from the patterns of particle collisions. Particle accelerators allow physicists to study the behaviour and nature of subatomic particles by propelling them at high speeds in powerful magnetic fields and then tracing the interactions that result from collision—enabling them to delve into the mysteries of the universe: the nature of dark matter, plasma, and the deep structure of space and time. These particle mandalas represent the phenomenal power and energy that is embedded in Nature and, like a mirror, reflects the powerhouse of humanity waiting to be released. Power is total and complete in and of itself, making no demands; it instead gives energy and supplies and supports and sustains. Its inferior cousin, force, takes it away, incomplete, and always needs to be fed energy from the outside. Power, being whole, needs nothing.

The feminine archetype, supremely courageous (heartfelt) in the face of daunting odds, knows how to embrace and accept that which otherwise could be lethal and dangerous. She understands the power of acceptance, trusts it wholeheartedly, and, from experience, knows that when we face our fears, when we face and bring light to our shadows, they disappear. That's not to say that she doesn't feel fear, merely that she feels it and acts anyway. Hers is the courage, for instance, to face another day when life has tried to crush her spirit, casting her hopes, dreams, and even those she loves into the void. The courage to be in the chaos and meaningless of it all, to be in the abyss of life, where nothing makes sense. This is the inner strength required when war and natural disasters bring chaos to family and communities, when war crimes seemingly destroy all sense of respect and hope. The strength to carry on, with power and integrity, however dreadful the circumstances; love yoked with the power of passion. The Strength card therefore suggests that you have the capacity to endure and overcome the obstacles that are presenting themselves to you right now. By calming the negative voices with the breath, witnessing the self-talk as a stream of consciousness rather than "the truth," you give yourself space to breathe new love. It speaks of being aware and acknowledging the instinctual energies that want to lash out and rage at the injustices of life, and tempering them from the inner well of love, compassion, and kindness. It asks you to relinquish your doubts, realign with your principles and courage, and thus reveal your true inner strength.

Reversed: You can't maintain control any longer; feelings of being overwhelmed, exhaustion, discomfort, agitation, even despair—a collapse. It's a tough time for you, so breathe deeply and come into the present moment, simply observing. Help is at hand as you are gradually able to recognise and acknowledge the different colours and intensities of your feelings, finding and locating them within your body. Explore somatic ways to transform and release them, such as singing, yoga, dance, running, simply moving. Use your journal to bring greater awareness to thought patterns and the negative loops that persist if you fight against them, rather than witnessing them.

SUMMARY

STRENGTH:

The courage to bring light to the shadows of fear and exist in the chaos. Relinquish your doubts—you have the power to endure and overcome any obstacles with love, compassion, and kindness. **Reversed:** Feeling weak, despairing, and a failure with insurmountable problems, you are not alone! Take a deep breath, observe, recognise, and acknowledge the feverish dance of your emotions. Come into the freedom of the present.

IX / THE ALIEN (HERMIT):

BRING BACK KNOWLEDGE FROM DISTANT PLACES.

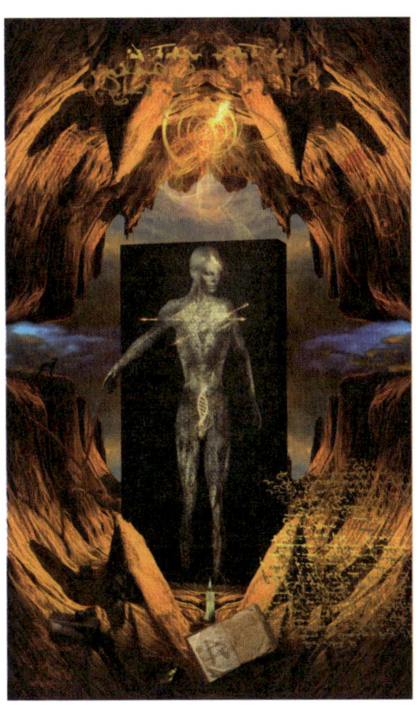

In the *Starman Tarot*, the Alien replaces the Hermit card, which traditionally invites the receiver to turn their attention inward in the act of contemplation and inquiry, to retreat from life and ask the big questions. The Alien is different. He arrives from the void with ideas, wisdoms, and technologies, a translucent presence, glowing with the sacred geometries and universal pattern of the Flower of Life. The figure of the alien has moved away from cults into the mainstream of popular culture, their symbolism continually evolving, often a repository for the fears and phobias of a segmented and disconnected population. Sometimes they appear as messengers from another dimension to guide or inform us of something important. As we become increasingly immersed in the "gleaming hyperbolic" digital reality, it is easy to lose sight of deep, meaningful human interactions. With the promise of seemingly endless ways to connect, we have never been lonelier and more isolated as a culture. Overwhelmed with information and content, we aren't able to distinguish truth from falsehood, verify the source, and understand the context in which it arose. We feel confused, disempowered, and a nagging sense of alienation. In a world where distance or remoteness enables and creates space for imaginary lives, snapshots of "the good life," all glowing smiles, it can be easy to feel like a failure and not part of the gang. We simply don't belong. This

Alien, though, is here to lead you back home to yourself. The Alien, the outsider, the rebel, the stranger, the one you have feared yet also secretly desired, is here to remind you that you are perfect as you are, beneath the mask of cruel imperfection. He invites you to take a break, to unplug from the din and the blue light of a screen, to reconnect with the "light" inside, the preternatural light of spirit. He represents your own hidden or lost wonder and miraculous powers—the parts of you that have become "alien" to you. In the difficulties of life, learning the rules and consequences of family, school, work, and relationships, parts of ourselves must remain hidden, suppressed, denied. Parts of the whole remain hidden and unknown. The Alien signals your urge for freedom. Naked and untainted, there are no masks; there is no great cover-up. He catalyses self-discovery and ignites the drive to question, challenge, and dissolve the walls that box us in. There is a remembering . . . the semblance of something more astonishing, more beautiful, and utterly remarkable surfacing. The rekindling of dreams . . . new possibilities . . . new worlds. He invites you to weave your earthly wisdom into new forms and expressions that have never existed before. He lifts you way above what you thought was possible, way beyond what you thought was "you," lifting you out of your personality and its defences and placing you back into yourself, whole, complete. The Alien, who carries spectacular visions and wonders, must always seek a way home to the stars—the light from afar—being in this world but not of it—reminding you that you are always, no matter what, on a journey back home to the light.

Reversed: It is time to come in from the cold and engage with the world, putting your insights and skills to work. The tendency is to hide, to shrink away from the risk of living fully. Unwilling to be truly seen. Lingering on regrets and past failures. Fear of success. Having shut yourself away, believing yourself to be powerless, dislocated, and at odds with society, it's time to make your way back into the garden of reality, bearing your gifts. There is much that needs transforming in every domain, so take your pick and set to work one step at a time.

SUMMARY

THE ALIEN:

The deep journey within the psyche, to sit with oneself and contemplate existence and the meaning of life. Rediscover your lost wonder and miraculous powers—the parts of you that have become alien to you. **Reversed:** The time of retreat is over; come share your insights and bear your gifts.

X / THE WHEEL OF LIFE:

I UNDERSTAND THERE IS A TIME AND SEASON FOR EVERYTHING.

The only truth is change; like the seasons, our lives are in constant (r)evolution. The Wheel of Life shows us that every living thing is in full cycle, from birth, and then death followed by rebirth. The law of conservation of energy states that the energy of a closed system must remain constant. Our universe is that closed system, so that the energy in existence has always been the same. Nothing is ever gained or lost. The forms that energy takes, however, are constantly changing. The artwork depicts a vast wheel surrounded by ghostly figures. It symbolises the personality journeying through time with all its different facets—the dramas of who we pretend to be—the different parts of ourselves that struggle for dominion in a world that operates on the principle of scarcity. The belief that there is not enough produces such struggle, such suffering. The ghosts of the past and the ghosts of the future dance to the great wheel of Time. Searching out who we were, what we said, what might have been, seeking where to go, what might occur. The mind, ever restless, analysing, commenting, distancing itself from the heart. We are always projecting "ourselves" onto life out there. However, viewed through the lens at the centre, the all-seeing eye reminds us that there is a constant unchanging centre to all changing phenomena. It's true our lives are in a constant process of change and evolution. Every project, person, business, government,

and country is birthed, matures, and dies. Much as we try to control our lives, nothing stays the same, and death and decay must come to us all. All the movement, the striving and relinquishing, causes such pain and discomfort because it takes us out of the present. The present moment when everything is just as it is . . . spacious, yielding if only we could let it be so. This is the centre of the Wheel of Life. When we open ourselves to the aliveness of the present moment, all is unfolding perfectly in the mystery of life. We expand and receive the "whole"ness of the moment, poised, alert, utterly alive. We wholeheartedly accept what is—love what is—without judgment, meeting the "isness" of the moment. In such moments we have no wish for it to be different or better or more; we have no disappointment, no sense that it is not what we worked for. Nothing to be, nothing to do, nowhere to go, this moment is complete unto itself, untainted, unmeasured. We shift perspectives from playing a character or role in life to the space in which life occurs. This card also reminds us then that what appears positive and uplifting contains the seed of its opposite, so that whenever something major changes in our circumstance, not to become overly attached to the outcome. You've met the man of your dreams . . . how wonderful . . . maybe yes, maybe no. You've moved to your dream house in the country . . . lucky you . . . maybe yes, maybe no. There is opportunity in everything, brilliance in everything, the cup overflowing with life, in everything.

Reversed: There is the suggestion that now may not be an auspicious time for beginning something new, for delays and setbacks are seen, with a possible fall from grace. Like the ocean, though, the tide will turn and come back in. Keep paddling, relax, and be patient. Perhaps it is a wise investment of your time to investigate what will really rock your boat? What is deserving of your resources, passion, and life force?

SUMMARY

THE WHEEL OF LIFE:

The only truth is Change; like the seasons, our lives are in constant evolution, the positive containing the seed of the opposite, so do not become overly attached to the outcome. Open yourself to the aliveness and mystery of the present moment. **Reversed:** Caught up in negativity, know it will pass; relax and prepare patiently for a clear direction to move forward.

XI / JUSTICE:

I REAP WHAT I SOW; I CHOOSE TO WALK THE PATH OF TRUTH.

Justice invites us to consider that we are the powerful orchestrators of our lives and that all of our thoughts, feelings, and actions have led us to the place we find ourselves in right now. It brings to light the principle of "consequences"—that which has resulted from your actions. Are you reaping what you have sowed? In the card, the figure of a woman stands upright—strong—wild—unapologetic. A universal figure of mixed origins stands holding a brain in one hand, a heart in the other, portraying the balance of head and heart, thought and feeling. The temple around her is teeming with life force, seething with symbols, futuristic, ancient, mystical. This card calls you to consider that balance of head and heart, logic and feeling, getting things done versus emotional well-being. To live well, to work well, we need both—a dynamic interplay and feedback loop between the two, helping us be efficient and effective, appreciative and purposeful. After all, emotion is a much more powerful driver of human behaviour than reason and logic alone. Justice invites you to take an honest inventory of your life and acknowledge your successes and defeats. You are the judge and juror because only you know in your heart of hearts if you have acted fairly toward yourself and others. If not, perhaps now is the time to regain integrity and make amends. Renewed power, autonomy, and freedom are revealed when we take full responsibility and give up making others wrong, life wrong. Remember that the finger of blame points one finger

forward and three back toward ourselves. In blaming others and life itself for our circumstances, we miss the opportunity to take back the power we have given away. We miss deliberating on the actions that could catalyse an amazing new lease on life and play the victim instead, stuck in the suffering. Personal justice, then, is what you know is right, balanced in both head and heart. It calls you to powerfully question that what you "know" at the deepest level is unjust. There are times in life when you must stand up for what is right for you—your own truth, and times when you must stand up for those who have no one to help them receive justice. This card is the great questioner, seeking out the truth and refusing to accept things that don't work or cause suffering and discomfort. It is the reclaiming of power from things that have been taken against your will or without your knowledge. It asks you bluntly what do you actually stand for; what are you willing to take a stand for? We live in a society and abide by rules and regulations we may not always agree with but have to navigate, for fear of the consequences. There are grave injustices in this world, escalating inequalities and marked polarities, especially in countries vulnerable to despots and warfare. While so many feel powerless in the face of their oppressors, the justice system in a democracy is designed to maintain order and bring balance, stability, harmony, and agency to its peoples, despite contrasting ideas about what is fair and equitable. The court of law recognises that there are fundamental inalienable rights that a person is entitled to, simply because they are a human being. Justice here calls you to recognise that your personal opinion of justice within the mundane world may be filled with contradictions, and yet, despite this, you must rise up and be guided by the Spiritual. Each action tips the balance either toward love or suffering, good and evil, right and wrong.

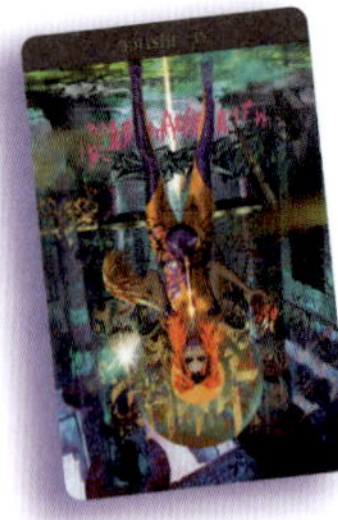

Reversed: Some form of injustice is at hand; maintain your balance and equanimity. Take response-ability and look to your own integrity. You may be caught up in disputes, and the incessant need to complain. Realise that the energy of complaining turns you into a victim. Seek to alchemise what you perceive as unfair, finding a way to transform the challenges or wrongdoings into valuable opportunities.

SUMMARY

JUSTICE:

The principle of consequences and spiritual law, gifting us the opportunity to create good or bad. You are being questioned about your integrity and the stand you wish to take in life. Seek out the truth and refuse to accept things that don't work or cause suffering and discomfort. **Reversed:** Feeling the sting of injustice in the world, how can you take responsibility and maintain the balance of head and heart, logic and intuition?

XII / THE HANGED MAN:

I NOW SURRENDER, THY WILL BE DONE.

We are hanging in the balance—no matter how much conscious and concerted effort we are putting into moving things ahead, it is so often one step forward, two steps back, an incredibly frustrating and disheartening experience. Depicted here as an upside-down, theatrical confidence trickster, an artful dodger and raconteur, the Hanged Man has lived successfully by his wits until now. Life has caught up with him; trapped, suspended upside down, he is seen hanging with a weight at his head, dangling over a precipice. The lightning that is stringing him up is symbolic of the power of Nature to intercede. Life has a habit of intervening to show us where we are out of balance, to wake us up and bring us back to our senses. The drive to survive, to push our limits, to succeed no matter what, trying to control life, pushing against life, very often results in life pushing back. The unconscious will often presents the imbalance in our dreams as a warning, and if we repeatedly don't listen, it will stop us in our tracks. Our health suddenly fails or we have an accident so that we are literally forced to stop and take stock. In the artwork the Hanged Man is losing the gold, the riches that have filled his pockets, the falling away of all that he has acquired and accumulated. Caught by lightning, he is in a precarious position; should he struggle, he'll very likely come crashing down to Earth. Resistance is futile; when our lives are turned completely

upside down by events, we are forced to surrender. It's no time to become impatient and negative, digging deeply into failings, but, rather, give up the struggle—there is little we can do out there in the physical world to shape our destiny; instead we must go within and make peace with ourselves. Hanging upside down, life is seen differently, akin to the practise of a yoga inversion: the blood flow is reversed, flowing back to the heart, and we feel it differently too. He is dangling upside down, with lightning flaring at his feet, and physical pain may also be a pathway into the body and his vulnerability. Vipassana meditation, one of India's most ancient meditation disciplines, which uses the breath to scan the body, is powerful in reshaping the perception of pain, physical or mental, as merely a transient sensation. This too shall pass . . . this card suggests that you are being forced to take time out and look at your life from a different perspective, reconnecting with your bodily intelligence and heart, leaving external concerns. Travel within, question, and ponder the greater spiritual principles and laws that are in motion; valuable lessons are there to be learned. Voluntary sacrifice, giving up the chase of worldly goods and experiences; significance and power may arise; the survival of the egoic self is handed over to the higher self for a "selfless" purpose. Freedom becomes possible when your life is in service to something greater, something of higher value.

Reversed: Life has been suspended for some time. Underachieving, avoiding what you know must be done, procrastinating, refusing to take responsibility. Efforts to change the circumstances of your life are repeatedly failing, and you are missing the opportunity to go within and listen to your inner voice, which is being drowned out by all the drama. It's no easy task to take a good, brutally honest look at your life, but it must be done if you want to regain your integrity, to make a difference, taking actions that will add value to the world. Journey within through meditation to receive insight and renew your trust in yourself and the process of life.

SUMMARY

THE HANGED MAN:

Turning things on their head, seeing new perspectives, letting go of your obsession with pushing forward and control. Forced to surrender; go within; make peace with yourself, others, the past; and discover the power of acceptance. **Reversed:** Life has been suspended for too long. Stop struggling; wait for your inner voice and fresh insight. Renew your trust in the process of life.

XIII / DEATH:

I KNOW THAT THIS TOO SHALL PASS.

This highly revered card does not signify physical death but, rather, heralds the death of a particular situation externally or part of you, internally. Like all major transitions, it brings with it substantial amounts of grief, anxiety, hopelessness, and fear. The end of a chapter in life can be hard to accept, but accept it you must if you wish to move on. This card depicts the ghostly resonance of an inhabited skeleton floating in space, an abstract environment with golden mathematical patterns, nature, numbers, flowers, and other symbols that indicate transformation. The skull and withered leaves denote death and decay, the life and juice sucked out of form. The brilliant and seductive orchid blossoms represent regeneration—virility, sexuality, and fertility; the potent visual, sensory language of flowers. Death and Birth are twins, intimately linked; we can't have one without the other; they work together; one leads to the other and the presence of one calls to the presence of the other. The symbol of the "Reaper's" scythe can be seen as harvesting the crop of valuable life experiences to be fed back into consciousness, so that it can better know itself. In a very real sense, we are living the cycles of death and rebirth all the time; every night when we sleep, we experience a mini death; the dissolution of awareness of the physical body makes way for the mental dream body, which then dissolves to enter deep sleep, silent, empty awareness. On his

deathbed the great philosopher Socrates exhorted his followers to practise dying as the highest form of wisdom. The Tibetans don't view life as we do in the West, a straight line from a to b; rather, it's seen as a full circle where birth and death connect with one another like an electricity circuit that conducts energy. According to most branches of religion and mystical tradition, it is the soul, the repository of integrity and neutrality as witness, that continues or transmigrates beyond death. The spinning mind with its myriad needs, wants, and worldly concerns is left behind with the body, at death. This card indicates that sudden and unexpected change is imminent; the ending of a major phase or aspect of your life is to be trusted. Death is the master cleanser. If you surrender to the process of dissolution, the letting go of situations and ways of being that you have outgrown, allowing it to unfold naturally, there will be much new growth, new life. We can use death as a catalyst to awaken to life. Ponder, for example, how you would live life if you knew you were going to die in a year's time. What authentic risks would you take, what conversations would you have? *A Year to Live* by Stephen Levine suggests that we don't wait for a death sentence. With every breath you take, someone in the world dies. Death, darkness, and difficulty are needed as much as light, ease, and flow.

Reversed: Stuckness and stagnation, living in the past and refusing to move on. Fear and mistrust; everything will be swept away; a sense that life is meaningless. Stop resisting, let go and let be, sacrifice the dream of what it "should be." Ask deeper questions that seek out the great miracles sitting beneath the surface of this transient reality. Alternatively, you may be resurfacing refreshed after a period of "dead time."

SUMMARY

DEATH:

The sudden death of a situation or state of being in life elicits grief, anxiety, and fear. Allow the emotions, seek wise council, connect with beauty, and gently let the transition birth new life. **Reversed:** Continued stagnation, reluctance to change. Stop living in the past and refusing to move on. Begin to make new plans, seeds that will grow into a meaningful future.

XIV / TEMPERANCE:
I AM ASTONISHED BY THE BEAUTY OF LIFE IN ALL ITS FACETS.

Temperance brings respite after the storm, a soothing balm in any situation. It suggests that when we take the time to balance the various elements and energies in our lives, we will find a clear pathway to our goals. This card embodies the nature of healing and moderation, self-care, and self-knowledge. We become whole when we acknowledge the different shades and colours of our personalities, understand their needs, and accept them. We cease the internal struggle and stop arguing with reality. If we know the exact blend of energy required for any given situation, we can walk with peace. Traditionally, the artwork visualises a maiden standing at the edge of a pool, one foot on land, one in the water, pouring the water of life from one cup to another. The cups represent the subconscious, intuitive powers and the superconscious, universal god mind, and the water blends their realities and ideals. The *Starman Tarot* is different: a strongly perceptive, androgynous being floating in the universe—a time slice of frozen light, delicate and fleeting—energy and form rising and falling, captured in midflight. The two female figures at the head are holding the whole scene in balance, so finely held and attuned that one slight shift either way and the image would collapse in on itself. For one second, everything is in balance; the exquisite is revealed, then disappears. Reminding us that we ourselves are frozen light moving through space that too will

quickly disappear. A reference to the Kirlian photography that was used in Bowie's *Earthling* artwork captures the phenomenon of glowing, coloured, electrical coronal discharges, the auras surrounding all living things. This card indicates that you have integrated many hard-won lessons and have a lovely degree of maturity and wisdom, consciously learning how to balance and calmly address the different elements, values, and priorities in your life. Slowing down, you too can capture the majesty of life, the extraordinary in the ordinary. A time of rebirth; seeing with fresh eyes, you marvel at the miracle and beauty of creation all around you and acknowledge that the pain you have endured in life was a necessary catalyst for this freedom. You are releasing the past and stepping deliberately into the present, aware of the dance and union of opposing forces, light and dark with the Divine. Your inner voice is guiding you; trust it—responding to challenges with restraint, flexibility, and a deep commitment to success. This is a brilliant time to combine forces and work with others because you have the steady, balancing temperament that can bring out the synergies between others with a magical mix of talent, experience, ability, and skill.

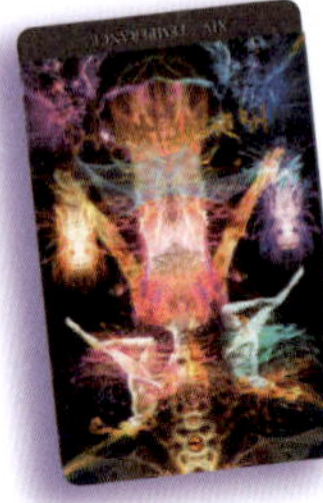

Reversed: Impulsive and unwilling to delay gratification. The desire for instant results and immediate pleasure at a cost, living life as if there is no tomorrow. Feeling disillusioned that there is a dull disregard for the long-term consequences of your actions, causing unhappiness and imbalance deep down. Consider what aspects of life or the personality need to be pruned and consciously released, allowing you to steadily move ahead, gently bringing renewed purpose to life.

SUMMARY

TEMPERANCE:

The exquisite order and wonder of life where different elements settle into a balanced, magickal relationship with one another. A special time to understand your own healing process and work in synergy with others toward a singular goal. **Reversed:** Living impulsively; disregard for consequences is causing imbalance and unhappiness. Seek wise council; work with the body to help consciously release what no longer serves you and move ahead.

XV / THE DEVIL:

I AM THE FALSE LIGHT, THE GREAT SPOILER; IT'S TIME TO BREAK THE SPELL.

Our concepts of evil—what is wrong, antilife—have shifted through the tides of culture. The Devil's character is one of the most demanding and complex, evolving from an "accuser" or "prosecutor" in ancient texts to a fully mythologised figure of ultimate evil and rebellion against divine order.

In the *Starman Tarot*, the Devil is a potent symbol of the great "spoiler of life." He is the corrupted "brilliance of being," a dazzling force that sabotages and seduces, running counter to life's natural rhythms. He sows discord, feeding on fear and suffering. We see him as an ultrafantastical, huge-winged "Angel of False Light," so hypnotic and alluring, we are transfixed—mesmerized by a beauty fashioned from fear and separation. That corrupted brilliance seeps into our DNA, even in the womb, waiting to be triggered.

This "false light" saturates our culture. We sense it in glowing screens, in the "glinting" illusion of digital life. There, we encounter smiling faces of loved ones juxtaposed with war, greed, and pornography. The Devil—corrupt brilliance incarnate—devours natural beauty. Our Great Mother Earth is mined, poisoned, and defiled for profit and gain. Oceans are emptied. Creatures slaughtered in the machinery of industrial food—paving a path lines with cruelty and disease.

It is the obsession with money that rewards the few while billions struggle. It's a tsunami of mental illness in the young, and the silent exile of our elders. It is the voice in our heads—mocking, jealous, and relentlessly cruel.

The radiance carries a petulant promise: liberation from time, from death, and from suffering. But stare long enought into that shimmer and what gazes back is not divinity, but our deepest fears, addictions, and limitations. The Devil—so astounding to behold—drinks the world dry of magick, beauty, and love, leaving behind a wasteland of synthetic pleasure and spiritual amnesia. And still, we remain spellbound.

Trapped in forgetfulness, we inhabit our lives stripped of spirit, rapture, and meaning. Artificial intelligence may soon know more about humanity than we can possibly comprehend, and yet remain utterly ignorant of the soul. This false light offers a superhuman mind devoid of heart, art emptied of the sacred, relationships without commitment, words without truth, and an unrelenting drive for more, more, more.

Yet, amidst this hollow splendour, a portal opens. A vital invitation arises: to reimagine your life—not as something inherited or prescribed, but as your own miraculous conversation with existence. The encrypted potential of your being waits to be activated, but you must choose to engage it. By familiarising ourselves with the corrupted brilliance, we can transform it through the alchemy of connection and compassion. Together, we can cocreate a world—and technologies that honour life, support the soul, and rekindle the sacred.

Seeing through the Devil's illusion, we return to the miracle of being alive. We cherish our bodies and honour time not as a tyrant but as a sculptor of meaning. This is not denial—it is awakening. We become a living presence of the eternal light of Love. An in this act of becoming, the Devil is transfigured—no erased, but transformed into a formidable teacher, whose fire forges us into something true, radiant, and free.

Reversed: Engaging in deceitful, manipulative, and possibly addictive behaviour that can bring misery and pain to yourself and others. Beware of envy and jealousy with the urge to sabotage the good fortune of others for revenge, personal gain, and gratification. It's time to uncover your insecurities, paying particular attention to your own negative self-talk. Keep a daily journal and practise gratitude to rebuild your confidence and integrity.

SUMMARY

THE DEVIL:

The dazzling allure of material success and power at the expense of integrity and one's higher values. The punishing goad in your head that keeps you awake. Something is gravely out of balance. It's time to shine light on the darkness and obsessions that grip our culture and pollute our minds; you must bring your spirit back to life by rekindling the sacredness of life—your life. **Reversed:** Continuing to engage in destructive and addictive behaviour. Notice the pull and allure of negativity; be vigilant as you redefine your priorities and self-worth.

XVI / THE TOWER:

I KNOW THAT RADICAL TRANSFORMATION IS BEING REQUIRED OF ME.

The Tower is visualised here as a steampunk industrial edifice that has colonised nature and is built within a Neolithic stone circle constituted from many found here in Britain. Part ancient and mysterious, part Burning Man installation, its summit bears a transmitter beaming man's existence out into space. It represents humanity's evolution and manifest expression: his ascent from working harmoniously with nature, through engineering and the organisation of industry, to the expansion, agility, and creativity of the radio telescope searching deep space, extending our vision of life beyond earth's limits. Fiery meteors are showering down, dangerously striking the Tower and setting it alight, symbolising the ultimate precarious nature of humanity. Like the dinosaurs, we too can disappear overnight; the things we've painstakingly built can be wiped out—our culture, our ideas, and the tangible evidence of it, razed to the ground. On a personal level, the Tower then illustrates how our belief systems and ideas constructed over time to form a concrete identity and picture of reality can seemingly be catastrophically demolished. The sudden force from outside or dark secret revealed and the story of who we are and where we're going come crashing down. The figures leap artfully from the Tower, a surrendered quality and grace to their descent, ambiguously hinting that perhaps, after all, they might not die, a metaphor for our capacity to

surrender to the will of nature. There is great power and freedom in "not knowing," in admitting the truth, overturning the conditioning that covers up the "I don't knows." Without precognition we cannot possibly know what's going to happen in the future; we can only guess at one, on the basis of assumptions. We don't know what's best for ourselves, and for anybody else, for that matter, including our children. This card signals there will be rapid, unsettling change in your life, accompanied by a sense that things are collapsing and falling apart; indeed, breaking down in order for something new to happen. In the long term, this shattering of internal and external structures can be an amazing catalyst for growth and wisdom—that which isn't true is blasted clean away. Change is not disastrous and earth shattering; rather, it is the leap from one thing to another. All the world's a stage; you look out and see the drama unfolding and look within to see the theatre of your minds; the only constant, change. Ultimately the Tower, which represents the structure and potency of the ego, is made of thoughts, so its collapse enables us to see and thoughts when truly seen are neither good or bad . . .

Reversed: Delaying the onslaught and destruction—prolonging the inevitable. Narrowly averting disaster. Deep down, you yearn for big change and transformation but are frightened of the terrible inconvenience. You can handle it—time to take the leap . . . risk . . . free yourself from the comfort of worldly attachments and securities and discover renewed meaning and purpose.

SUMMARY

THE TOWER:

The collapse of old ways of being, thinking—knowing. A striking personal revelation that destroys ignorance and demands a radically new approach. Whether tragic or euphoric, the lightning flash delivers a sudden shattering break with "normal" reality—a difficult yet amazing catalyst for growth. **Reversed:** Delaying the inevitable, catastrophe is heading your way if you continue. Wake up! Take an honest look at things; begin to rebuild from solid foundations.

XVII / THE STAR:
I BEAM YOUR LIGHT.

The figure is graceful, arms raised above her head, hands delicately poised, reminiscent of the beautiful sacred dancing that is performed at the temple rituals and cultural dances of Bali. Her fingers conduct fine electric filaments, divine energy, as she stands in waters boasting much aquatic life. Hands reach out to her from the depths below, and her starlight nourishes and raises them out of the sea of overwhelming emotion. The Star, a potent symbol of light and transformation, pierces the mask of the ordinary to release the extraordinary. A powerful conduit of the Divine radiance, she moves effortlessly between the personal and transpersonal realms, embodying and transmitting energy that is larger than life, fully cognisant that she is a divine vehicle and catalyst for the star energy in others. She lives in the incredible freedom and expansion that the energy offers her, and trusts it completely. Her Presence is felt, charismatic, a great lightning conductor. Working with Bowie, perceived by so many as the ultimate Rock Star and consummate performer, I saw someone profoundly interested in the human condition. He shone the light on other people and their talents and gave people a real platform on which to shine. He was unconcerned with fame and fortune, and I experienced him as an enabler, an intellectual, and a generalist who had a finger in every pie, clearly understanding the dynamics of what he asked people to do, open,

humble, and always willing to learn. He seemed to have a tremendous thirst for knowledge, drawing from fields as diverse as art, philosophy, spirituality, literature, history, and anthropology with extraordinary focus and discipline to refine and reveal the truth of the work. So often in life we see the Star up onstage shining their light, forgetting about the tremendous focus, determination, self-control, and sacrifice that is required to light up the world for us. Starlight travels through time and space, the emissary of the celestial realm, a pure source of creative flow igniting inspiration. This card therefore indicates that this Star quality is available to you—the extraordinary that lights up the ordinary, exposing the magic that is always available in your life. A renewed sense of purpose and creativity suggests that it's time to reveal your hidden talents and shine brightly. There is much you can offer that will be gratefully received.

Reversed: Lacking inspiration, your creative sparkle has drained away. Despondent, with little acknowledgment of your creative abilities, you've lost faith and direction. It's possible that you are still feeling the tremors and fallout of the Tower, and you are being invited to look again at your foundations to see if they are indeed solid, and then begin digging for that vein of creative sparkle. Nourishing physical practices, foods, rituals, creative dates, and attentiveness to your creative heroes and heroines will serve you well.

SUMMARY

THE STAR:

The emissary of the celestial realm guides you through the chaos of life, illuminating the path to your highest potential. Sensitive to the shifts and play of your own inner needs and emotions, know that you have the inner resources—inner light—to live life on your own terms and shine brightly. **Reversed:** Deflated, despondent, loss of purpose and vital spark. Shine the brilliance of hope upon your lost dreams, revise and reimagine, illuminate your purpose.

XVIII / THE MOON:

I PERCEIVE THE TRUTH THROUGH THE INNER VEIL AND ITS REFLECTION.

The Moon signifies journeying within to the pool of inner wisdom that the subconscious inhabits. The moon is the light that shines in the darkness, and her waxing and waning mirror the movements and tides of our emotions. Seen here, she is the woman in the moon shining her gentle light over the waters below. The Moon is in synchronous rotation with the earth, meaning that the same side is always facing the earth, and the gravitational pull that the moon exerts creates the two bulges on the earth, which move around the oceans as the earth rotates, causing the familiar high and low tides. Women's menstruation cycles often harmonise with the cycles of the moon, and in the times of goddess worship more than five thousand years ago, women would often bleed together on the new moon, considered an auspicious, deeply creative and spiritual period of release, and then ovulate at the height of their creative release, the full moon. Living life can be a very lonely path at times, especially when we are transitioning from the old to the new. The path unknown before us can be laden with projected fears and fantasies of loss and failure, but the Moon card suggests looking a little deeper into your life, past and present, to face your fears. It is time to retreat and reflect, attentive to the synchronicities and symbolic wisdom in the outer world reflecting in the mirror of the inner world. Allow insights and guidance to surface in your dreams,

and keep your dream diary ready. Remember we can feel our most desperate or despondent in the darkness, given to flights of the imagination, twisted fears, and fantasy. As mistress of illusion, the dreaming self, she holds both the keys and the spells. Deep forgotten memories may be disturbing your equilibrium, past traumas resurfacing once again to experience the light of consciousness—the healing spiral. You perhaps thought that certain issues were resolved, but up they come again to be purified in the moonlight. Journey within, using the power of guided visualisation, and like the three ethereal water bearers in the card, ask and receive her wisdom. Success in any venture always carries fear as it does hope, the two sides of the same coin. Darkness cannot exist without light, light without dark . . . embrace your fears.

Reversed: Buried memories may be unravelling, spawning an overactive imagination as you consider a new phase of your journey. Have courage; danger does not lurk at every corner; you must go on. Look to the Moon—the pathway of healing, compassion, and self-care. Ground yourself with fresh, nourishing, and preferably "whole foods" and a physical practise such as yoga, Pilates, or tai chi that attends to the body. Allow spring or distilled water to purify you of negativity and fear.

SUMMARY

THE MOON:

The symbolic wisdom and mysterious intelligence surfacing in dreams, meditative creations, and imaginings want to be acknowledged and integrated. Memory traces, long forgotten, rise to be purified, unlocking fears and projections, to be released into the cleansing flow of Mother Nature. **Reversed:** Plagued by imaginings of loss and failure, deep insecurities, lack of sensuality. Bathe in the Moon's tender healing waters, the feeling, fluidity of life, self-nourishment, and care to release the wellspring and root of well-being.

XIX / THE SUN:

I CONNECT WITH THE LOVE THAT ILLUMINATES MY HIGHEST POTENTIAL.

The essence of the Sun card was gifted to me in a beguiling, rapturous experience whilst walking in bright sunshine. Suddenly, the sun became utterly iridescent, streams of beautific colours beaming down to kiss the earth, and I found myself enveloped in a thick, preternatural light that vibrated with a spiritual presence of unimaginable wisdom and intelligence. Two golden spirals of light hovering in front of me conveyed a soft yet immensely powerful communication, gifting me understandings of the spiritual reality of light and plasma—the intelligence and miracle that is the source of all life on Earth. I could intimately "feel" the sun speaking to Life in a lexicon of colour frequencies. As this experience ripened, an image of a stunning Sun Goddess blossomed into my imagination; in fact, it was beyond imagination, something I cannot accurately put into words. I instantly knew this had to be the remastered card! The Sun Goddess was holding the "seed of life" in her hand, which radiated a dazzling light infused with what can only be described as the geometry of Love—a wild, rapturous Love that could become anything, everything. It was as if the sun—our sun—was enacting the miracle of shaping the eternal light of Love into form, living forms. I was left completely in awe by what I had experienced and understood. Beyond the pragmatic layers of science, light entering your eyes is an aspect of what can be

called "original magic"; the ancient, radiant mind of a star flows within you through the gift of its light. Each one of us has the capacity to connect with the light wisdom and magic that is alive in both our sun and the light from countless distant stars caressing/framing the earth. This is what can be called "the radiant mind." We can first connect to this aspect of mind through the light of our consciousness when we take a moment to place our focus on the simple experience of "being." As we practice this one simple thing, it becomes apparent that our "sense of being" is not blank/ hollow, but, rather, the softest, most beautiful light radiates from the very core of our being, a flow of love and ultimately guidance. This guidance can take shape as images in your mind's eye, or like a delicate whisper of meaningful words. Importantly, this communication has a different "quality" from normal thoughts, emotions, and images. As you pay close attention these aspects, carry a "luminosity," an integrity that the normal chattering thoughts lack. This guidance from the sacred light is what we call intuition—I prefer INNER-TUITION, and unique pathways to express that original magic in everyday life become greatly enhanced and illuminated. The "light" of our consciousness is amplified, and we can reveal here on Earth the miraculous wish for life that stars are constantly transmitting to us. It is time for us once again to see the stars as deities, with their unique and mighty stellar form of consciousness. Know this: The light that flows within your entire body—through every atom, your mitochondria, every cell—carries the language of stars. Take a moment to simply connect to the radiance that infuses your body, your mind, and the world. Tune in to this radiance and your light—your living potential—will be revealed. Allow this light energy to infuse your words, how you speak about yourself, and life in general. As you go deeper, you will find that you can declare who you are and the promise your life contains. The Sun card is a call for you to illuminate a vibrant life vision, fully expressing all the colours of your unique persona.

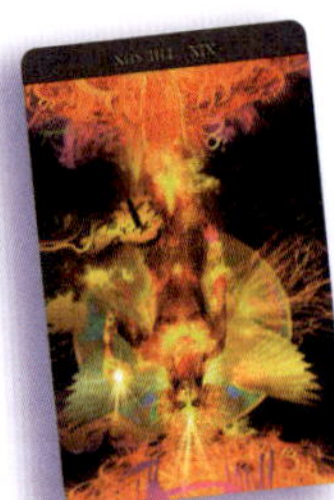

Reversed: Your light and energy have grown dim, and you have lost sight of your dreams and a powerful vision for your life. You have forgotten how beautiful this world can be, how exciting life can be. Reconnect with the sun, bask in its rays, and notice how its warmth and light bring all forms to life, the patterns, and intricate geometries. Open your eyes; allow the light into your body. Begin crafting an inspiring life vision, open to the miraculous, and remember you are from stars.

SUMMARY

THE SUN:

The sun heralds warmth and the sheer visceral celebration of life. Laughter erupts; fears and regrets dissipate. A beautiful new vision comes to light, enriched with meaning. An exciting period of natural growth and expansion, the bountiful fruit of your labours flourish. **Reversed:** Too good to be true? Cynical and resigned to life not being fair. Don't let the negative clouds dim your radiance; seek out beauty; don't take yourself too seriously.

XX / JUDGEMENT:

I AM VIBRANTLY ALIVE AND LIVE INTO THE GOD/GODDESS THAT I AM.

The powerful figure, arms raised, has just received the force of Divine revelation. Struck by an epiphany, he is instantly transformed, transfigured into a luminous, space-age preacher. The metamorphosis is complete—an unrecognisable embodiment of spiritual revelation, his previous life wiped clean. The rebirth is complete. He is compelled to live differently—to change everything about life at once; there is no going back. The energy transmitted by this revelation raises the dead and the skeletons are brought back to life, alluding to the far-reaching regenerative power of revelation. We are awakened from the hypnotic quality, the spell of the habitual and restricted being and doing in life—just getting by. In an instant we realise that something fundamental must change. We recognise the lie that we have been living; the "story" about ourselves and life is seen for what it is. The meanings that we have carried from childhood, the assumptions we have made, the lens passed on to us, through which to view life. That part of us that was lost or has been hiding or lying dormant is now revealed and must be lived out, fully expressed in the world. We are called to action. The revelation wasn't asked for, wasn't sought; rather, it was bluntly administered. There is no choice but to act upon it. Awake to something entirely different about life, a compelling new possibility; we can't go back. This is a highly charged card, not always easy to receive,

and yet, it carries huge significance and potency. It charges you with the task of looking without hesitation into your life, to see what has been buried, is unloved, and is calling you to bring it to life. The life you had been living was comfortable, perhaps, but it is not the full truth of who you are and why you are here. Already you quickly recognise the recurrent themes, dynamics, and patterns of your life and have a clear picture of where you were heading. Signalling a new holism, the events and patterns of your past, like the pieces of a jigsaw, have come together to form a whole, complete. In a flash, all can be understood. All is forgiven. You forgive yourself. That phase is over and you are transformed, free to live into a greater reality, a more expansive potential. Stripped clean of all the limitations, old beliefs, and experiences of the past, you can see into your own future with fresh eyes. Judgement calls you to be the visionary for yourself. Expect change to naturally unfurl as you revision your life in a whole new way.

Reversed: Something is clouding your judgment, erring on the side of caution, deflated, afraid to make the next move. Look at the personal pattern of judging and self-blame; pay attention to the transpersonal patterns of judgment and blame woven into our social structure of family, religion, law, economy, and class. Harness the energy and momentum instead for something worthy and life sustaining.

SUMMARY

JUDGEMENT:

The greater patterns of life synchronise to bring you sharp focus, clarity, and understanding. A sudden, great revelation. Unfinished business, stuck energy, can be resolved and cleared. You are fully awake and alive to your creative potential. **Reversed:** Cautious to harness your energy for something worthwhile, you are sapped of passion and enthusiasm, snared by the false prophets of material wealth and superficial distractions.

XXI / THE WORLD:

UNIVERSE, I AM YOUR BELOVED CONDUIT FOR THE RADIANCE AND GRACE OF LIFE.

We meet the piercing gaze of the Earth Shamanka warrioress, standing resolute, fully present. She rises out of the ground, embodying the immense force of Mother Nature. She is a wise, ancient Being, and the magic of alchemy and sacred earth mystery are woven into her crafted armour, worn with powerful elegance. Around her is the skeleton of industry, a former factory, now transformed by Nature into some great cathedral or temple. The world in all its forms is her church. The twisted branches reaching into the space represent the ancient bristlecone pines, the oldest nonclonal organisms on this planet. In forests, recent research has suggested that the biggest and therefore oldest of the trees, now known as "mother trees," have vast mycorrhizal networks of fungi below ground that support young trees or seedlings, preferentially ferrying them the nutrients they need to grow. The ancient Mother Tree is a recurrent theme or motif of the *Starman Tarot*, delivering the energy of the miraculous tree, ancient, rooted in the wild earth, having lived through so many epochs, an ever-present witness to the stream of life that has come and gone. It reminds us to respect and honour nature that is so formidably strong, for her presence will prevail no matter what we think and say about saving the planet. Behind the Earth Shamanka looms an image of the world, the earth, half encased in a metallic shell to represent humanity's encroachment upon

the sacred mechanisms of Nature. At the apex sits the great Tree of Life, receiving the light communication that will restore and heal. Mother Nature always decides and stands as the shamanka, unapologetic, displaying her defences. Although considerably advanced in years, she remains vital and potent, provocatively sensual and fecund. She exhibits her fertility with handfuls of grain, and the cacao pods laid out before her, sacred food of the gods, which originated in South America many thousands of years ago, are some of the most complex and nutritiously dense foods in existence. She gifts us her abundance freely and offers us one of the greatest treasures of all—the royal metal, the gold ingot, fashioned into astonishing artefacts for millennia. Gold was, above all, sacred to the sun deities, kept in trust by the priesthood and used in ceremony and ritual to maintain the balance and harmony of nature. In return, there is an offering of the sacred medicine plant, tobacco whose smoke carries all thoughts, feelings, and prayers to Mother Earth Shamanka and the Creator of the World. This card is highly auspicious and invites success in any endeavour if you walk the path of integrity and offer your work and projects in service of humanity and the earth. You are finally mastering life and are literally taking the World by storm. As a clear vessel and channel unfazed by the tumultuous changes and cycles of life, you tenderly and expertly balance these compelling and natural energies. Earth, water, fire, air—the elementals are experienced as marvellous instruments that can be played together to make exquisite music and harmony that resounds through the universe. It is time to gather your tribe and be a force for good and the sacred beauty of this world we have been gifted to create on.

Reversed: Deserved success is short lived, tainted, for there is much to do and a bigger mountain to climb. There is a disconnect from the World and the life-giving and sustaining force of Nature. You must bring yourself into alignment with Mother Nature, her rhythms and her healing, taking great care of your physical body. It's time to pray and offer gratitude for all that nurtures and sustains you.

SUMMARY

THE WORLD:

A triumphant celebration resulting from patiently and expertly navigating the complex terrains of life, offering your work and life as a sacred gift. Understanding the true origin of fear and pain, you have the experience and wisdom to build and share something of value. Balancing Nature's elementals, you are a potent, refined conduit for a timely vision. **Reversed:** Disconnected from the natural rhythms of Mother Nature, forgetting the lessons of the past, unable to sustain success. Reconnect with the wisdom of the ancestors, build upon what works, and practice gratitude and ritual.

THE COURT CARDS

WANDS

PRINCESS OF WANDS *(Earthy Part of Fire)*

I SPARK THE IMPOSSIBLE.

A sun child, she dazzles all who meet her, young, free, and formidable. In her presence, nothing is "impossible"—she wipes us clean of past fears, so that we can create in a space of pure freedom. Her luminosity resonates, sparking a memory that we (and all of life) are light bound up in matter. Her fire fuelled by breath (air) transmutes the heavy energy of past experience and failure, burning it clear away to release light energy. This potency can catalyse a new vision, and she is honoured as a brilliant initiator. The art for this card arises out of my teenage interest in science fiction and the elaborate fantastical imagery that sought to express equally complex psychological concepts. Jean-Claude Forest's comic strip of the '60s, *Barbarella*, with its sexually charged and mystical planetary realms, evoked the fiery tantric space goddess. The

idea of space being a vast, exotic, and erotic realm was always so alluring, instead of the dry textbook versions. Space is utterly dynamic, a vast, untold mystery of light and geometry becoming infinite forms and expressions. For me, the Princess of Wands epitomises our capacity to infuse our reality with a mythological quality. In a similar vein, the illustrations of superheroine Octobriana, said to embody the principles of the Russian Revolution and battle against both Russian and American oppression, was a character that both I and Bowie cited when discussing how to visualise "Ramona A. Stone" for the *Outside* album book. The Princess of Wands transmits the drive to experiment and innovate. It is about death of the old and birth of the new. It is in letting go of fixed beliefs about how something "should" be that we are teleported into an open realm of pure potential. Cast your doubts and fears into the fire to be melted down and transformed. Allow the exuberance of youthful confidence and innocence to surge. You can consciously take on something that appears to be impossible, and flourish and grow in the challenge.

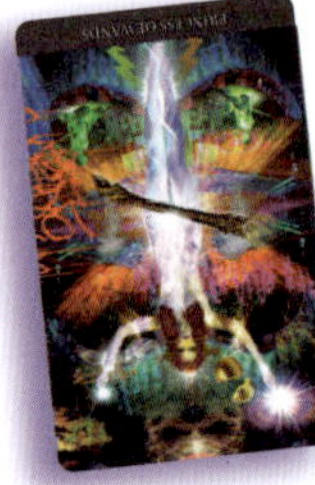

Reversed: Just as we can find joy and freedom in the improvisation of life, we can also find ourselves sparking too many ideas and projects, constantly stuck in the process of conceptualising or overwhelmed with busyness. Too much restless, purposeless activity leads to frustration, indecision, and diminished confidence. Slow down, balance, and ground this abundant vitality with good "wholesome" nutrition and holistic practise such as yoga, qigong, or tai chi or outdoor physical activity such as parkour or running in nature.

SUMMARY

PRINCESS OF WANDS:

The spark of energy, abundant with tantalising ideas, ready to embark on a marvellous adventure. A fire has been lit, your passion ignited, and despite fear and trepidation, it is time to prepare for success. **Reversed:** Sparking too many ideas or too much action, slow down and ground your vitality.

PRINCE OF WANDS *(Airy Part of Fire)*

I PASSIONATELY SET OUT TO CONQUER.

This young prince is hot-blooded and hotheaded, bringing huge passion, action, and courage to everything that he encounters. He is dashing and dynamic, and our hearts positively brim with excitement should he blaze into our lives. However, his daredevil, explosively progressive actions may leave a trail of burnt debris as he relentlessly pursues his triumphs. Nothing will hold him back, and he's quick to flash you a grin and stride forward, fearless to the end. Often regarded as a revolutionary, he is the archetypal athletic hero set to conquer a despicable enemy or despot. He has unquenchable self-belief and, as a true visionary and adventurer, believes that he can change the world and should be lauded for doing so. The impetuous, youthful male possesses all the necessary prowess and skill but is not experienced or seasoned enough to wield them with absolute skill and precision. I see him as a long-haired youth, part Ziggy-like alien, larger than life, bringing a message of hope, attired in his splendid, retro-future armour. He is surely too dazzling to be hurt. Yet, in the dark realms of life, he must face being hurt; his youthful splendour will be vanquished by life and the passage of time—a great sadness. Nevertheless, there is something astonishing about the hero, the freedom fighter who, without a second's thought, will face the most formidable adversary. I remember friends of mine joining the army, barely men, imbued with the

passion to actively seek out danger and test their mettle. One in particular, a lithe, boyishly good-looking hero, an elite green berry, never made it back from the Falklands Conflict in '82. At nineteen it seemed impossible that someone so dazzling and young could perish in the mud of a distant land. Despite the flurry of excitement at the appearance of the prince, the great catalyser, this card for me, then, is a kind of "warning" not to rush into things. Don't be fooled, though; war is the least likely cause of death of the young and valiant; road accidents followed by suicides are the biggest robbers of life of our princes. (Youth is notoriously bad at assessing risk, so eager are they to seize life by the scruff of the neck.) The key here is to use the Prince of Wand's fiery colour, exuberance, and sheer courageous zest for life, skillfully. Take on the entrepreneurial spirit and leap, think big, and believe that you can conquer. Be the one to stand up and speak out for change, to determinedly and fearlessly pursue your dreams; after all, you get only one shot at life.

Reversed: The magical, synchronistic, and amazing energy of the prince has disappeared and been replaced by restlessness, anxiety, and a serious depletion of energy. The natural "highs" of the prince have turned to "lows." Focus on rest, relaxation, fitness, and a nourishing diet of food and positivity, creating the space to plan and properly illuminate your ideas. Without decent fuel (earth—physical and air, thought), your flame will be extinguished.

SUMMARY

PRINCE OF WANDS:

The archetypal athletic hero is set to overcome a despicable enemy, and it's time for you to take a bold leap, think big, and believe the impossible is possible. **Reversed:** Restless, impetuous, and undisciplined or depletion of vitality; step back, move ahead with your eyes open, and think things through carefully.

QUEEN OF WANDS *(Watery Part of Fire)*

I GRACEFULLY TAKE CENTRE STAGE.

This queen is a force to be reckoned with: bold, daring, courageous, and extremely vivacious. Highly versatile and talented, she is passionate about the world she lives in and the domain she rules. She sees that the needs of her people are of paramount importance, and does her very best to envisage powerful solutions, thereby highlighting and pursuing many just causes. I created this card while thinking about the powerful feminine visionary, a beautiful balance of head and heart. Flanked by a court of transfigured Minoan mother goddesses, she symbolises the power of the feminine principle to give life, reminding us to speak with the fire of passion and the integrity of the heart. The radical anthropologist Chris Knight puts forward a powerful argument that women were key to our human mastery of complex language. That it was the deep connection of women regularly coming together at the time of their cycle and their development of complicated systems of herbal medicine used, for example, in childbirth that catalysed the complexity of interpersonal communication. The power of words to create our reality, emerging from our female ancestors. A fiery and spirited mother, she encourages her children to be bold individuals, ambitious and discerning, to speak up and act on their feelings. Beneath the skirt of the Queen of Wands, she wears a Union Jack petticoat, a playful reference to the *Earthling* artwork I created

for Bowie in which he wears an Alexander McQueen Union Jack coat. The emblem of Britain, so prolifically and provocatively used across music and fashion movements, with mixed, paradoxical meanings. Similarly, she is the visionary designer, the unapologetic experimenter, eclectic, charismatic, and supremely confident about freeing people from their normal perceptions, routines, and habits. Flanked by two black panthers, fierce guardians and the symbol of the mother, the dark moon, and the power of the night, these totem animals encourage us to understand the power within shadows, to pierce the veil of darkness, face the unknown, and discover the field of pure potential. She welcomes you to expand your awareness, affirm yourself, and be resolute, taking the time to consciously nourish your self-confidence and self-esteem. It is time to remind yourself of all those past successes and triumphs, harness that get-up-and-go attitude, and audaciously take centre stage in your life.

Reversed: An overbearing, domineering, manipulative temperament has been adopted to get your own way. Designing for a number of years within the music business, I experienced how the creative ego shines when taking centre stage, then craves the "highs" outside the arena. Unless grounded in nourishing relationships and routines, integrity, that inner sense of wholeness can be easily lost in the pursuit of fame and fortune.

SUMMARY

QUEEN OF WANDS:

The wonderful balance of head and heart, she is a compelling visionary force to be reckoned with. Lean into your confidence and charisma; trust your intelligence and heart. **Reversed:** Overbearing and controlling or generous to a fault; reconnect to your own needs and get clear about your highest values.

KING OF WANDS *(Fiery Part of Fire)*

I SEEK TO CHANGE THE WORLD.

Of all the kings, the King of Wands is the charismatic ruler of his people. Descended from the lineage of the Iatromantis, ancient shaman-prophets who practiced a magickal technique called incubation, allowing access to the fourth state of consciousness—consciousness itself—where extraordinary acts of creation and manipulation of the physical world could be actualised. This king is an imposing, inspiring figure; he is the archetypal man of action, with unbelievable reserves of energy, creativity, and vitality. He is masterful in not only initiating change but applying the discipline needed to see it through to its fruitful end. The king symbolises phenomenal inner strength, courage, and leadership and, understanding the volatility of fire, is able to harness its force for the good of all. The King of Wands has always been a very powerful card for me, symbolising the ability to disrupt in a truly creative and peaceful way. His body is made from aromatic, resin-coated kindling, the heartwood that is found in the stumps of ancient longleaf pines, which blazes hot and bright and, if well organised, builds the foundation of something that burns long and well. The king in ancient times was perceived as a god, the crown often spiked like the rays of the Sun God. This king wears a crown of thorns, an emblem of conscious humility, for his authority is rooted in the manifest world. His wand creates new forms of life, symbolising just

how powerful the human imagination is—we create our own reality. He stands before the magical furnace of imagination and creativity, where new contexts are forged into reality. The creative process begins with generation, so don't be too quick to discard your ideas; let things grow before you decide what must be pruned back. Working with Bowie, I was constantly reminded that every aspect of a design or artistic creation contains the potential to be a game changer. I experienced him as phenomenally disciplined, relentless in keeping the integrity of the vision, able to zoom in on a detail that would be seen as insignificant and to coax something significant from it. At the same time, I was struck by how affirmative and generous he was to others, encouraging them to shine despite being phenomenally busy and constantly in demand. Likewise, the King of Wands is a mentor to those around him, especially his children; coaching them to reach their full potential is of supreme importance whatever his work schedule and obligations. His world is exciting and action packed, and he will encourage his children to use their initiative, take risks, and go out and explore the world. This for me is the essence of leadership; to be totally committed and direct in your purpose and at the same time giving others the opportunity to be fully birthed as the person they carry the potential to be.

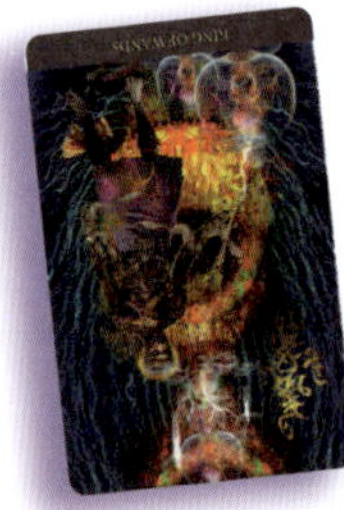

Reversed: The king may be channelling too much fire and given to argue, dominate, and create drama all around him. He has become absurdly arrogant and authoritarian, critical and unforgiving. He doesn't encourage other people to flourish; rather, he micromanages and puts everyone on edge. Creativity is stunted. Remember to play your highest game in life but always maintain a sense of humility and be willing to learn from those around you—everyone is your teacher.

SUMMARY

KING OF WANDS:

The inspired charismatic ruler, catalysing change and applying much-needed discipline, wisdom, and generosity to fruitful ends. Your enterprising spirit sees tangible opportunities for success and leadership. **Reversed:** Dominating and arrogant or overwhelmed and indecisive; need to redress imbalances, gain clarity, and reprioritise.

PRINCESS OF CUPS *(Earthy Part of Water)*

I OFFER YOU ARTISTIC BEAUTY.

A gentle, delicate being, the Princess of Cups is finely tuned to the fluid realm of emotions. Perhaps naively, she wants to believe that a utopia is possible, a world that is abundant with love, light, and peace. When she discovers that the world can be a dark and deadly realm, the shock reverberates deeply into the core of her being until it's almost unbearable. How can human beings commit such acts of negligence, hatred, and terror? How can they embody so much anger and ill will? Her bandaged eyes symbolise the unwillingness to witness the suffering, and instead she must look inward. Her strategy is to develop a fantasy world populated by gentle, radiant beings and creatures who are continually moved to love, support, and nurture one another. Her "imagined" consorts stand by her firm and unmoving. A world where love is given and received unconditionally, and all forms of life are affirmed and cared for. As a

child of the Spirit world, where everything is evolving to its purist potential, she is able to commune with this vast domain of knowledge and accumulated karmic wisdom that, for most, remains unconscious. She resides in a deep temple—ancient/futuristic—rich with symbolic meaning, where the light of the unconscious mind is carefully ported through a black mirror. She therefore resides both in the seen and unseen worlds and can be a powerful messenger, using her perceptive nature and sensitivity to visualise and evoke the archetypal transitions and journeying that we all face in life, in an endeavour to come home and become "whole." When we allow the hurts and challenges of life to make us a more inspiring, loving, and beautiful human being, we are walking the most miraculous path. This is the alchemical game of transforming our burdens, the ball and chain of life we carry, into radiant possibilities, to move through life with grace. Not to allow ourselves to be soured by sadness or be held in the withering grasp of regret is a constant practice, and one worth fully taking on. This card invites you to consider how a complaint, when looked at from a different creative angle, is transformed into a rich form of guidance.

Reversed: Devastation and heartbreak are experienced when you see the ugliness of life, the sheer ignorance and self-destruction in humanity, but without the capacity to transform it. Stuck in an uninspiring world, surrounded by mediocrity, you walk through this grey world and become lost, losing your sensitivity and sense of wonder. No longer capable of being surprised or delighted by something, you will need to lick and nurse your wounds, but creativity is a worthy ally here, enabling you to fully release and express the depth of your feeling.

SUMMARY

PRINCESS OF CUPS:

The sensitive one, intuitive, perceptive, and profoundly spiritual, she signals the opportunity to develop and refine your own "inner-tuition" and creative talent. **Reversed:** Loss of sensitivity, devastation, and heartbreak; recovery through nourishing your creative spirit through art, beautiful words, healing sound, and movement.

PRINCE OF CUPS *(Airy Part of Water)*

I ARTFULLY NEGOTIATE FOR THE BEST SOLUTION.

The Prince of Cups is the archetypal Knight Gallant, a gentleman in every sense: honourable, considerate, valiant, and noble. Not one to relish violence and battle on any level, he far prefers behind-the-scenes diplomacy, but if he must, he will act swiftly and cleanly to achieve the best results for all. A masterful peacemaker and artful negotiator, he is always looking for the win-win solution to problems, and his caring, compassionate presence can be a very welcome alternative to bloodshed. He admirably carries and balances the feminine, feeling, and receptive side of his nature alongside the fast, focused, and powerful aspect of himself, the masculine that is ready for the call to action. That action is inclusive of his feelings, making him a fine, loyal, trustworthy, and supportive friend and family member. His watery temperament enables him to bring a measured, reflective pace to his activities and duties; the one exception is the area of romantic love, where his passion can seize the day and see him leap headlong blazing. He will shift hell and high water to "rescue" the one he loves. Intensely romantic and sensual, he risks much heartbreak and raw pain on his path to true love. In essence I see his character as the grail seeker, the untainted romantic where life is filled with the possibility of discovery. The manta ray—flying through the ocean, navigating the different depths—teaches us how to dig within ourselves and observe our emotions

with a calm gracefulness honouring the different levels of our being and the world around us. It takes real effort and concentration—even courage—to keep a flame of exuberance alive in our hearts. Instead of seeing ourselves adrift in a hostile world, we can look and see that everything carries a message to guide us to our most powerful possibility. This in essence is the elixir, the medicine, the Holy Grail—not an object with miraculous powers; rather, a way of being in the world. Once you begin to see things this way, the world literally changes before your eyes. As we travel through life, it's an immense challenge not to be caught in the trap of cynicism. Yet, to become cynical and resigned to the "way things are" brutally robs us of our life force. Most of us reach a point when we must consciously choose and, what's more, create a discipline of consciously choosing. Albert Einstein suggested that we examine the most fundamental nature of life when he said, "The most important question you can ever ask is if the world is a friendly place." Every time we resign ourselves to the opposite, we leave behind the spark of life that can be astounded by something new and unexpected.

Reversed: You may be experiencing some form of emotional confusion and turbulence, seesawing between tremendous hope and delight one minute, and abject despair and disappointment the next. This card suggests that your imagination may be getting the better of you, and it would be advisable to take stock of your situation and regroup. It invites a calm, reflective approach, a chance to fill your own cup from within and logically consider your options.

SUMMARY

PRINCE OF CUPS:

The dashing diplomat and artful negotiator who strives to win the best solutions for all, he invites a sensual, measured, romantic, and reflective stance. **Reversed:** Emotional confusion or unrequited love requiring self-nourishment and building mental discipline.

QUEEN OF CUPS *(Watery Part of Water)*

I AM A CONDUIT FOR POWERFUL LOVE.

The sensual, dynamic healer, intuitive, sexual, and otherworldly, she demonstrates your gift of emotional intelligence, a rich empathy, creativity, and understanding. Creating the Queen of Cups was a truly joyful experience. This archetype resounded so richly in my mind, symbolising the possibility that life is in fact brimming with a magical energy and that we have simply forgotten how to see it, experience it. I wanted to bring out the animistic nature of this Queen card. Animism, from the Latin word *anima*, "breath, spirit, soul," is the belief that objects, places, and all creatures possess a distinct spiritual essence—even words can be infused with spirit. We see the old broken television, releasing a spirit into the waiting cup as an Ibis-Woman reaches for it in reverence. It refers to the Egyptian belief that birds had a special magical power: flight . . . the possible source of our image of winged spirits, angels. The entire environment of this card is vibrantly alive and interactive. Sticks become tiny "Alberto Giacometti" beings, busying themselves around the queen, an idea replicated in children's stories such as Pinocchio, where the wooden puppet eventually turns into a fully fledged human boy. Again and again we see life—consciousness—emanating from mere wood or metal, little glass girls in fairy tales, toys coming to life when adults leave the room. In this context, we can fully accept the life in normally inanimate

objects, and yet, we forget that the chair we sit on is made from the same "energy" as us: All life springs from the same source and is animated by the same energy. Animism is a theme that I would be drawn back to throughout this Tarot deck. The idea that ordinary things can become conduits of the miraculous plays out strongly in this card—the extraordinary in the ordinary. We are all, in fact, miraculous forms of technology, spirit technology. The fact that, as of yet, science still has no idea of why we possess consciousness tells us that life is so much more mysterious than we can possibly imagine. To connect with the wonder of your own existence is the path back home. This card is therefore concerned with matters of the heart and signals acceptance and a rich empathy and understanding of the nature of things. To feel your inherent empathy with your fellow creatures, to be emotionally intelligent and fully expressed, unashamed of what your imagination is capable of conjuring. There is much to be gained from listening deeply within, giving credence to the dreaming world and being a bridge between the two.

Reversed: Overwhelming flow of emotions may be dragging you down, eliciting a strong urge for distraction—a guru, spiritual ideal, exercise, plant medicines—rather than facing up to responsibilities. That which initially relieves the pain in turn becomes the source and a bitter medicine indeed. Excavate the past, surfing the rhythm of grief, feeling the patterns, and discover the root of your pain, likely sewed in childhood.

SUMMARY

QUEEN OF CUPS:

The sensual, dynamic healer, intuitive, sexual, and otherworldly, she demonstrates your gift of emotional intelligence, a rich empathy, creativity, and inherent understanding of what is good. **Reversed:** Overwhelmingness and addictive distraction; lovingly feel into the root of your discomfort and use meditation and fluid movement practices such as tai chi or dance.

KING OF CUPS (*Fiery Part of Water)*

I BRING PEACE AND HARMONY.

The king travels through his kingdom, appreciating this watery realm that brings such life and sustenance. Water's transformative properties are utterly unique; its ability to freeze, melt, evaporate, heat, sublimate, and combine with so many elements makes it the ultimate shape-shifter. Our bodies even create a special type of water called "structured water" or "exclusion zone water" (EZ water), a fourth phase that has truly magical properties, such as creating "free" energy from light. The king is the master of the water element, able to control and discipline his emotional viscosity, a man totally at ease with life. He is portrayed here as an old Rastafarian shaman smoking his pipe, always in good spirits. He has great command of the animistic realm, believing in the supernatural power that organises and animates the material universe. He is hovering over the ocean, sitting on his car craft throne, a unique creation, and the decrepit, burnt-out car has been upcycled into something extraordinary, reflecting his capacity to redefine and reconstitute discarded or dangerous elements into something of value. Over time he has developed immense emotional intelligence, able to access and bridge the conscious and subconscious realms, fully aware of his connection to the Divine Source. Listening calmly to its guidance, he brings a great, timeless perspective to unfolding events and acts as a diplomat and wise counsellor to his people, enabling

his kingdom to live in peace and harmony. This same gentle, compassionate, and tolerant nature is directed toward his family, and his presence as a father is abundantly amiable, creative, and attentive without being unboundaried. Like the gift that keeps on giving, in his presence, anybody and anything can take on value—symbolised by the beam of light emanating from his power centre, which turns the liquid in the cup to gold. Wise and experienced, chilled, laid back, humorous, free spirited, and very creative—he is a jovial Neptune-like figure who's made his home in both worlds, land and sea. An arts connoisseur, he appreciates the power of the arts in all their forms to convey individual and collective life stories, both as a cause for celebration and as a cathartic release and purification. He will venture into places that are unfriendly, dark, and unpleasant and infuse them with good humour, embodying the ideal of polishing one's mind and body to foster a spirit of harmony—an aikido master, indeed. This card therefore suggests that a calm, creative, and wise influence is at hand. There is great inner strength to be accessed that brings with it a natural ease, grace, and joy. The unseen is seen, accepted, and beautifully expressed. Fear is dissolved in the elixir of harmony.

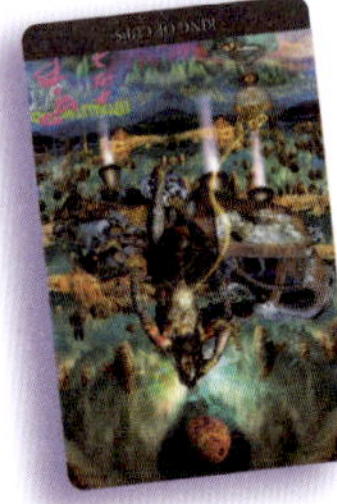

Reversed: The cup is lost, signalling the loss of this emotionally rich guiding system. Disconnected from the heart, thinking could quickly become unbalanced and confused, cold and distant. One would do well to retreat and use the power of nature to heal, especially connecting with the therapeutic qualities of water to cleanse, heal, and relax the body.

Summary

King of Cups:

The wise, solid counsel of someone who has mastered their emotions and seen everything, he suggests a calm, creative, and timeless wisdom calling forth your natural ease, grace, and joy. **Reversed:** Confusion or emotional distance registering the need for greater understanding of psychology and motivations.

PRINCESS OF SWORDS *(Earthy Part of Air)*

I CALL ON YOU TO LIVE YOUR TRUTH.

The princess holds her sword with relaxed confidence. She possesses an unwavering daring, with her domain high up above the city's streets, running and leaping across rooftops. She sits unfazed by the precariousness of life. Boasting both an agile young body and clear penetrating mind, she is a fabulous fusion of superheroine and freedom fighter, a princess with an unquenchable thirst for truth. Her nimble mind, grasping and connecting stimuli at lightning speed, gives her an incredible outlook and ability, a searing intelligence able to penetrate any circumstance, any drama, rooting out inconsistencies and delivering a powerful argument. Emotions don't get in her way as she almost marvels at the quickness of her own mind to instantly read a given situation, assimilating many facets and contrasting, comparing, synthesising, and evaluating possible solutions. It is almost a sport for her. Equally an avid raconteur, with a beautiful speaking voice and a wry wit, she draws out dilemmas, philosophies, and wisdom in

her storytelling that is way beyond her years. Her home is unashamedly in the sky, perched on the roofs of skyscrapers like some exotic creature out of a scene from *Blade Runner*. Ridley Scott's great sci-fi epic, which visually inspired a generation, is married with the animation of *Ghost in the Shell*, Japanese manga, science fiction with comic book. Her mind soars freely in the sky, rising and gliding like a bird on the warm vertical currents of air, giving her a unique and calm perspective. Up high, though, she can see that there are many other vistas to explore, and she won't hesitate to sharpen and test her sword on the most challenging of these. Inherently hardworking, principled, and knowledgeable, she will pitch her wits in the fight for equality and justice for all. You could be mistaken for thinking that this princess will indeed change something profound about the world. If only it were that simple. Those ideals, so beautifully articulated, could easily remain in the mental realm and not actually be grounded in reality. This card indicates that the brilliance of the mind is at your side, an agile advocate for cutting away any obstacles as you scale the heights to success. You may be called to review the set of principles and assumptions that you are living by, the high ideals that you are pursuing or once believed in. Life is a great journey filled with setbacks, wrong turns, and dead ends. You are being called to be an intrepid explorer, to question assumptions, values, and ideals. What is the purpose of your life? Why are you here? What do you want? How might you navigate the difficulties, the inequalities, and the dazzling array of opportunities to realise the best of your potential? What do you think is possible from the very best of human existence? The time is ripe for a philosophical reexamination of the "meaning" of life and a reacquaintance with some of the most remarkable thinkers and philosophers of our time. You are ready to begin walking your talk, embracing the risk of being alive.

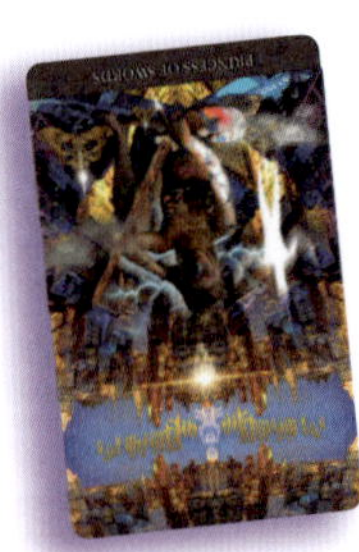

Reversed: Loss of the exquisite balance between air and earth; out of balance. The sharp cutting edge of the inner critic cuts away at confidence in one's abilities to solve problems and inflicts emotional injury to others. Disconnected from feelings and overwhelmed by thoughts and ideas, unable to focus and bring anything of real value to life. A physical practise such as yoga, dance, weight training, or flow rope would serve her to get out of the head and into the body, while remembering the importance of breaking down any goal into manageable steps.

SUMMARY

PRINCESS OF SWORDS:

The ardent raconteur—risk taker—whose agile young mind penetrates the dramas of life to uncover the facts, a great ally in revisiting the profound questions and purpose of life. **Reversed:** Sharp criticism with an emotional disconnect; an embodied grounding practice such as yoga or qigong is advisable.

PRINCE OF SWORDS *(Airy Part of Air)*

I LIVE BY MY IDEALS.

The ***prince*** is here, danger is imminent, and the time has come to act, now or never. The sword falling from his wounded hand, hovering, as if waiting to be grasped, a symbol of this commitment to action. Unyielding and dogmatically determined to follow his principles, he is willing to sacrifice himself for some lofty cause. He understands that this is a burden and will endure the hardship and punishment that may be inflicted as a consequence. His quest is ultimately exciting and relentless. To manifest things truly worth achieving, to protect or propagate the ideas or beliefs that we most value, will always demand that we surrender or destroy something we hold dear. The artwork for the *Starman Tarot* required that I work phenomenally long hours into the night for months on end, poring over the details of each card, constantly reworking them until I felt they captured the spirit of the deck. In the long, cold, grey winter months of a British winter that was particularly shocking after living in Bali, driven by what I understood as my Daemon to fully express the energy of the deck, I frequently felt like throwing in the towel . . . exhausted. However, from long experience I recognised that I was treading the tightrope—I knew there was something past the point of giving up. I summoned the willpower to imagine the good this project could generate, faces of people lighting up, the clarity and creative inspiration that was

received, and that rippling out into the world. Immediately I would revive—a surge of renewed energy and spark of inspiration that would carry me on. The breakthrough—a new vista would open up. The "I can" replaced "I can't." It's as if providence wants to make sure we are fully committed before gifting us the possibility of doing something extraordinary or beyond our normal capacity; our entire being is augmented toward something vital. To fight a cause when all appears lost, to be willing to go to the places that most terrify you, because you implicitly understand that something of tremendous value awaits, calls forth the vitas of life. In receiving this gift, we discover that "thought"—our small self—is no longer the prime faculty that determines our actions—we are guided by a higher power to do what must be done. The Prince of Swords embodies this energy, and the huge raven signifies the arrival of this vital force. The prince himself is modelled on an acquaintance, a young punk rocker who embodied the energy of the tragic rock icon, Sid Vicious. Heading for a similar untimely end until one night a drug score went horribly wrong, leaving him almost battered to death. That night he had a vision of Jesus telling him that he could give up, and it would be just fine, or he could go back into his life and help impact the lives of sick children. All the energy focused on the wrong cause could be redirected, transmuted. As soon as he was out of hospital, he set about getting fit, running races, and gaining sponsorship. Instead of vodka, he drank green juice; instead of hustling for drugs, he hustled corporations to contribute money for hospital equipment. He became unstoppable. To what is your energy being focused? What decisive action do you need to take?

Reversed: Too much fire and he quickly burns himself out. Too much air and his leadership will be overexacting and demanding, out of touch with reality and the life-giving principle of love. Constantly fighting for the wrong cause. Look closely, adjust course, ground your knowledge, and get behind a tangible objective that has real consequences for your local community; become unstoppable.

SUMMARY

PRINCE OF SWORDS:

The decisive action of an exhilarating mission; willing to sacrifice everything, you are being called to act, focusing and aiming your ideas with confidence and courage. But "first" you must be careful to choose your cause wisely. **Reversed:** Razor-sharp ideals are misdirected, overexacting, and ambitious, quickly burning themselves out. Slow down, gather your facts, and create a measured plan.

QUEEN OF SWORDS *(Watery Part of Air)*

I SERVE A NOBLE CAUSE.

In mythology, the Queen of Swords was often but rather simplistically conceived as the "Ice Queen." This highly intelligent, forthright, and principled woman is obliged to perform her tasks and duties as a monarch. She is not afraid for heads to roll if she needs to protect her own or her kingdom's interests, but the dark tears symbolise the sadness she bears as a consequence, for she is no lover of execution and death. To live in integrity, she would far rather build alliances with her adversaries rather than use brute force. She is dressed here in a Starman samurai kimono, representing self-discipline, courage, independence, honour, and willingness to serve her kingdom no matter what. As head of state, she offers excellent counsel and constructive criticism with a piercing intelligence and well-earned wisdom. Here, she handles sacred medicinal plants that have coevolved with human beings for millennia and been used by them for healing and guidance as part of spiritual practice. We eat plants, drink their juices, ferment and distil libations from them, and consume them in a thousand forms. While some are toxic, such as the berries of nightshade, holly, and dogwood, many have proved extraordinarily valuable. The use of herbal remedies, for example, goes back possibly hundreds of thousands of years, and today the majority of the world's population, an estimated five billion people, use folk medicine both for acute and chronic health

conditions. The queen's medicinal journeying enables her to cleanse herself of toxic thoughts and experiences, a form of spiritual cleansing restoring the mind-body connection, head with heart. Self-sufficient and perhaps a perfectionist, she is phenomenally capable, knowledgeable, and engaging, with a brilliant intellect that can penetrate to the source of a problem whatever the domain, personal, political, or corporate. Her keen intelligence quickly strips away what's not important, accurately reflecting the facts and uncovering priorities and values. In the process, she uses her own experiences to help illustrate and unmask self-defeating patterns, deeply understanding on all levels the importance of a stitch in time to save nine. She applies this rigorous effectiveness with her own children, regarding it as her maternal duty to see that her children grow up to be well-rounded, cultured, highly educated, and ethical adults. Not always the warmest of mothers because she carries the heavy burdens of duty, she does, however, bring compassion and a deep understanding of the vicissitudes and trials of life and is deeply committed to them contributing their gifts and talents effectively and making a difference in the world. See where you are putting off what must be done to create freedom and integrity; choose your actions for the good of all and fully commit.

Reversed: The queen is embittered; her searing intelligence, rather than being released exquisitely into the world to serve a noble ideal, is turned inward in terrible self-reproach or outward, to blame and criticism. Her emotional and intellectual intelligences are seriously out of balance; either a dried-out husk, her intellect lashing out to attack or destroy, devoid of the juiciness and fecundity of love and positive emotion, or flooded by emotions, she sinks into the mire of depression, paranoia, unable to see and think things through logically. Either way, she is in need of nurturing and deserving of the noble cause of self-care.

SUMMARY

QUEEN OF SWORDS:

The independent, formidable, and principled energy, taking no prisoners, willing to do what must be done. A phenomenal organiser and problem solver, she can guide you to live by your highest principles and not be pulled off course by doubters and naysayers. **Reversed:** A searing intellect that is thwarted by too little or too much emotion, in need of nurturing and reconnecting to ancient, feminine wisdom and healing.

KING OF SWORDS *(Fiery Part of Air)*

I BELIEVE IN A FAIR WORLD FOR ALL.

This serious, high-minded king sees it as his duty to rule and govern his kingdom with absolute fairness and equality. He gives scant attention to his emotional life, perceiving it to cloud his judgment when he has to make difficult decisions that affect people's lives and livelihoods. He is careful to foster an environment that resounds with positivity, supported by clear laws that nurture human dignity. Every human being, he believes, is born equal, an innocent, and has the right to be valued, respected, and treated ethically. He views it as the responsibility of a civilised society and its governance structure to foster the conditions whereby men and women alike have the opportunity to fully contribute and realise their potential. He knows that it poisons society and is horribly detrimental to us all when people are dehumanised, objectified, humiliated, or treated as a means to an end. He sits astride his throne, a monumental electric chair demonstrating his invincibility and tolerance of pain. A formidable intellect, fearless leader, and arbitrator, he is the consummate professional who calmly sizes up any situation with remarkable speed and accuracy, applying a hawk's-eye view of events and potentialities. The lunar module on fire shows that once a decision is made, there is no going back; he removes all escape routes with the same ingenuity

and energy as Alexander the Great. The mandrill baboon at his feet displays his choice of fierce, powerful allies, belying the fact that beneath the king's facade is a very sensitive, caring man. As a father he is perceived as cold and clinical, a firm disciplinarian and taskmaster, but underneath he loves his children deeply and only wants the very best for them. He regards it as his duty to raise his children into responsible, capable adults and citizens, able to use and exert their intellect while mastering their emotions, for the betterment of mankind. As a lover he is skilled, organised, and reliable, requiring his partner to be an intellectual equal while respecting his personal freedom and control. This card indicates that you are in the position to critically assess powerful situations around you, aligning them with your ethics and your belief that everyone should be given a fair chance to learn, grow, contribute, and prosper. Given a clear perspective, you can calmly formulate a workable plan and strategy to pursue an ideal, no matter what the obstacles. Putting emotional concerns to one side, it invites you to gather the facts and information and analyse them critically in order to put forward a logical, workable solution and resolution for all.

Reversed: You are feeling driven, impatient, and in no mood for time wasters. Punishing standards and judgments about incompetence are making things hard for yourself and others. This air of disillusionment and even despair needs to be dispelled. Overattachment to details—you need to rise and gain a fresh perspective, renew your focus, choose the people you surround yourself with wisely.

SUMMARY

KING OF SWORDS:

The highly scrupulous intellect that fosters a powerfully positive vision of humanity, willing to endure pain, destroy escape paths, and enlist the most-fearsome allies. Requires that you quell your emotions and come up with a workable plan of action. **Reversed:** Punishing standards and judgments about incompetence, disillusioned, requiring renewed focus. Step back and gather fresh resources and knowledge.

PRINCESS OF PENTACLES *(Earthy Part of Earth)*

I VALUE ALL OF LIFE.

A powerful synthesis of both the imaginative and practical, this discerning and hugely resourceful Princess of Pentacles is acutely aware of the responsibilities we share as custodians of this remarkable planet. Deeply committed to the principles of ecology and evolutionary biology, she wants to live as consciously as possible, innovating solutions that will sustain and restore the earth's living ecosystems. The bare trees represent the devastating ways that we are still poisoning the earth. She stands inside an old nuclear cooling tower, alluding to the controversies that surround nuclear power, and offers a way out, up the beanstalk. The sun at the summit reminds us that light is the key, from how we heal our bodies to how we power our cities. The Princess of Pentacles is an imposing figure, stunningly pregnant, fecund with the possibilities of

bringing the earth back to life, carrying the magical, grounding energy of the Pentacles suit. A strong carnivalesque and shamanic presence, she carries the didgeridoo, the world's oldest instrument, whose haunting, primal sound heals the land and its people with the power of breath. She is dressed like a magician with her cape, and the red shoes at her feet pay homage to Bowie's "Let's Dance." She doesn't risk being danced to death by their strange magic; neither does she want to draw attention to her high economic status and power, preferring to go barefoot, earthbound. She is deeply in tune with the principle of Gaia, that the earth can be regarded as a self-regulating organism, its elements of air, oceans, and land surface forming a complex, interrelated system that supports life. She values all of life in its rich diversity and believes that her patient work, ingeniously planned and executed, will lead to sustainable change in the future, carrying forth the wisdom of her ancestors and rebirthing it within this complex Information Age. While many in the previous generation have lost their way, bewitched by global media and an acquisitive lifestyle, she painfully sees the fruitlessness of that path: barren, polluting, devoid of the nourishment that so many yearned to fill themselves up with. Practical and ambitious, she is drawn to those who share her vision and industrious nature, often collaborating brilliantly to achieve long-term aims. Perhaps her ventures will be part of the hypothesised Imagination Age, where creativity and imagination, sustainably applied, become the primary creators of economic value. This card invites us to consider how we are making solid, grounded foundations and preparations for what we ultimately value and hope to achieve in life. It suggests that we have much in abundance already, and not to squander precious resources frivolously. She reminds us to seed, plant, and grow and nurture our vision, one step at a time.

Reversed: There is a loss of natural vitality, a disconnect from nature and its raw sustenance. An overattachment to creature comforts has sapped you of your strength and sense of purpose, and you are operating within your comfort zone. Step out, go barefoot, respond to nature, and don't get distracted by what's ultimately unimportant.

SUMMARY

PRINCESS OF PENTACLES:

The fertile combination of a sharp mind and vivid imagination. Controversial, eye-catching, and purposeful to bring a life-sustaining vision into being, supporting humanity's relationship with Nature and the sacred. **Reversed:** Stagnation and loss of natural vitality, overly concerned with trivia. Reconnect with what truly matters; dare to think and act differently.

PRINCE OF PENTACLES *(Airy Part of Earth)*

I CONSISTENTLY CREATE MY EMPIRE.

This youthful prince has the powerful and exacting combination of dynamic qualities, the air of the wild adventurer, together with the trusted stability, solidity, and rootedness of earth. Exact energetic opposites to one another, these elements invite ongoing tension, and he must work hard to balance and master them within himself as he heads out to discover and conquer the world. As a young prince, it is his duty to expand knowledge, resources, and boundaries while defending those territories already acquired, and the earthy part of his nature seeks new lands of opportunity. He sees that magic and alchemy are possible everywhere if he acts quickly, but he must marry this confidence and zest for life with the down-to-earth pragmatic side of himself. If he does so, he can accomplish a great deal. But we can become aware that there are other things happening within his domain that he has not seen, guiding us to keep an eye on the whole picture, seek out wise council, and not try to solve everything alone. He is seen here sitting on the back of his horse, a beautiful, intricately engineered animatronic, an incredible beast, embodying the force of nature combined with human ingenuity. The power of the horse, a universal symbol of freedom without restraint, when tamed, transformed people's mobility, freedom, and working lives. The prince's horse, poised like some great exhibit, symbolises the transition between serfdom and the Industrial

Age, the inanimate carrying the spirit of life. The appreciation of technological innovation is reminiscent of Prince Albert's vision to create the Great Exhibition in London in 1851, the first international exhibition of manufactured products, which was enormously influential on the development of so many aspects of society, including art-and-design education and international trade and relations. The profits of the exhibition went on to fund the world-renowned Science, Natural History, and Victoria and Albert Museums, which continue to inspire admiration and ingenuity in minds young and old today. The power of the pentacle is transmitted through sound technology that was first invented in the 1920s, the loudspeaker, and it plays the sound of the Starman. This card suggests that it would be prudent to map out a strategy for the next phase of your life adventure. The challenge is to discover practices that will keep your passion burning brightly and develop some form of patience. Focusing on tangible actions and time frames and accounting for resources will then take you masterfully toward your vision. Make your words sacred and do what you say.

Reversed: Too many details or weighed down by practicalities, the vision can be easily lost. Without consistent self-care, direction, and well-paced and well-placed energy, there could be burnout. It might also suggest tremendous hard work, but with a loss of ambition, in survival mode. Perhaps it's time to throw caution to the wind, shake away the scepticism, and step forward with a bolder vision.

SUMMARY

PRINCE OF PENTACLES:

The dynamism of adventure is tempered with stability, problem-solving, and precise action, indicating an opportune time for disciplined, focused plans to ensure the sustained success of a project. **Reversed:** Too many details or weighed down by practicalities, the vision is lost. Step back; connect with "why" you want something to happen.

QUEEN OF PENTACLES *(Watery Part of Earth)*

I LOVE AND NURTURE THIS GREAT LAND OF OURS.

This queen is the ultimate earth mother, the great healer. Mistress of Nature, she is the ultimate protector, nourisher, and sustainer of wildlife and their ecosystems. Her passionate connection to the miracle of life in all its forms has given her knowledge of the bountiful matrix; that everything is indeed connected to everything else, powered by the sun. She is the great channeller of the vitas—the life catalyser signified here by the fecund energy that streams from her hands, shooting life into the seedpod that releases the strand of DNA into the world. Utterly sensitive, sensual, and receptive, she is an abundant channel in this Garden of Eden. The small armadillo wearing its armour on its back is symbolic of protection, a physical and spiritual shield that guards its safety, indicating not only the need to protect the heart when the occasion calls, but reminding us humbly of how small we are in the scheme of life. This creature, who typically lives in subterranean dens, further prompts us to remember that Earth is the great womb and tomb of all life. We are all part of Mother Earth, an indivisible, living community of interconnected systems. Clearly in evidence is that the myriad of forms of exploitation and contamination over the years have led to corrosive deterioration and destruction, threatening the diversity of life, including our own. If we were boldly to proclaim as a Universal Declaration of Rights that the earth is Gaia, a living entity

that has the right to exist, persist, maintain, and regenerate its vital cycles, then might we not be catalysing the life force from the seedpod with our own hands? Legal power to prevent misguided interests from treating this earth as mere property to be sold to the highest bidder. Might it protect the gift of fresh, clean water—less than 3 percent of all water sources and, even more miraculously fragile, less than 0.01 percent of it, the surface water found in lakes, swamps, rivers, and streams? The armadillo's uncanny ability to walk underwater and then survive torrential flooding by inflating its body, so that it can float, reflects a way we ourselves might navigate the watery realm of emotions and surrender to its torrents. This queen is certainly moved to take action. Despite her considerable wealth and status, she is conscious of the precious opportunities and resources she can access in her daily life, and doesn't for one minute take them for granted. Aware that she has been afforded privileges that many in the developing world don't have, she realises that wealth for all can happen only when we engage our collective political and social will to distribute it fairly. You are being invited to connect with the natural abundance of nature that is your birthright, and to channel it beautifully to catalyse life. You are being invited to heal body and mind and to eat the most-energy-rich foods, bringing consciousness to how you walk and regenerate the earth.

Reversed: The queen has lost her cherished connection to Mother Earth and, as a result, is more than likely neglectful of herself, her environment, and those around her. Perhaps weighed down by the need for materiality, her self-esteem and status inextricably linked to her bank balance, she finds herself constantly working, striving for success at the expense of her health and relationships.

SUMMARY

QUEEN OF PENTACLES:

The great passionate protector, nourisher, and sustainer of the natural world, she brings heartfelt nourishment, resourceful solutions, and grounding to all aspects of life. **Reversed:** Disconnected from Nature, neglectful of self or overly attached to trappings of material wealth. Breathe deeply and fully, connect with sunlight, eat food with seeds, and walk slowly in Nature.

KING OF PENTACLES *(Fiery Part of Earth)*

I HAVE MASTERED THE ART OF SUCCESS.

This King has command of immense wealth and luxury for all to see, but he is not the typical empire builder; there are no glittering palaces and great monuments erected in his name. Rather, he seeks to transmit a love of life, nature in all its wild majesty, and employs his resources to enable future generations to take pleasure in it. The gold nuggets and golden symbols surrounding him show the riches gained when difficulties are overcome, the diligence and fortitude required to recover from setbacks and conquer. He understands that the more you prune back a tree, removing diseased, broken branches, thinning the crown and so increasing airflow, and letting only one dominant branch to grow, will enable the tree to create a strong, resilient structure capable of weathering the storms of life. His love of trees and natural materials with a strong refined aesthetic is experienced in his home, an eclectic showcase for the very best in local craftsmanship and design, bright, comfortable, lavish, and steeped in history. He is an avid collector of art and antiques and appreciates the workmanship, knowledge, and skill that has been passed down from father to son through the ages. His beloved throne from ancient Persia, the carved stone bull from Persepolis, expresses his strength. Beneath the flamboyant Zappa exterior lies a strong, powerful, hardworking dynamo. Some say he's paid a heavy price for success; a workaholic, he was often absent during

his children's formative years, but nevertheless he has always provided a stable, loving home. His children have received an excellent if unconventional education centred on the home, where the importance of nutrition and keeping the body active while attending to the balance and beauty of one's immediate environment has been instilled, nurturing both the physical body and the body of the earth. He knows that insecurity comes from the fear of collapse; the collapse of a situation, a business, a relationship, your life. He's also fond of saying that money doesn't grow on trees, and has endeavoured to teach the value and responsibility of really caring for things rather than treating them as disposable or replaceable. All resources are precious. Generous with both his time and money in these mature years, he's keen for his children to follow in his footsteps while also mentoring young creatives and entrepreneurs eager for success, encouraging a clear vision and a coherent strategy for their long-term goal. Think success, act success, and keep that vision grounded and alive, consistently working hard, persistently moving forward every single day, no matter what. As the vision grows stronger, and your focus remains strong, just as the pentacle appears to just fall into his hand, your life and success will appear to flow effortlessly.

Reversed: Come back down to earth, reassess your situation, and bring much-needed stability to your life. Those impeccably high standards of the upright king have been overturned, highlighting a need to revisit your foundations—the routines of your daily life that nourish and support you and the values that inspire you to be your best.

SUMMARY

KING OF PENTACLES:

The determined, fun-loving, yet steady and committed empire builder, aesthete, and lover of nature indicates success if your vision is anchored in being practical whilst fostering a sense of design and beauty. When these two energies are in unison, success becomes natural. **Reversed:** Feeling trapped by circumstances, stale, ungrounded. Take time to study how Nature puts things together and work accordingly.

MINOR ARCANA

WANDS

ACE OF WANDS

I AM THE CATALYST.

The Ace is filled with pure potential, the magical, combining, and creative element of fire. In the artwork, notice how the wand itself is pregnant with the potential of human life: the foetal stage of existence where anything is still possible. The twisted wood of this wand comes from a great Mother Tree, whose vast mycorrhizal network links itself to hundreds of other trees in the forest, passing nutrients such as carbon to feed her seedlings, for without wood there can be no fire. The wand is encased within a fiery coronal womb, as if it is waiting to be birthed in the vastness of deep space. You are a conduit, to be shaped by this immense heat, energy, and force. This card indicates the luminous sense of self-belief, self-esteem, and vision you have in this moment or

the immediate future. Don't let anything stand in your way as you resolutely step forward into the unknown. Fire burns brightly and will generate the highest and greatest of visionary aims and ambitions, but you are at the start of your journey, a novice, with much to learn and contend with. You must use the energy from this wand to build a well-ordered fire, tending to it carefully and using your ingenuity to keep it alight whatever the conditions, internally and externally. You must discover how to temper, train, and stoke its ever-flickering and changing flame; otherwise it will pull at you from many directions, tantalising and overwhelming you with every opportunity, taking you completely off course. There is the danger that you could also be drawn too close, bewitched by its mesmerising spell and suddenly seeing your goals and dreams consumed in the flames. You are therefore wise to familiarise yourself with each of the elements, air, earth, water, and fire, so that you might draw on their balancing energies and natural law. For example, the earth and stones, which keep the fire bound and contained, together with a calculated supply of fuel, represent the well-defined practices and habits that support body and mind, sustaining the flame of your vision rather than exhausting it, burning you to the ground in the process. Let the warmth and light illuminate your path. It may be appropriate to create a special, sacred space in your home, an altar, perhaps, to place symbolic objects, pictures, and words that will keep the flame of inspiration alight. Visualise yourself achieving your success—what will you feel, see, hear, sense? Create a "vision board" with your miracle project, whether it be career, romance, or planning a family or home at its centre, emanating streams of activity and magic into your life.

Reversed: Whereas the ace is a big "Yes, go for it!" signal, the reversed aspect points to delays and setbacks to an important project. Take a deep breath and review what's going on: your energy levels and your sense of purpose and whether this really is the correct project to take you forward. Frustrating, yes, but acting methodically will help ground your vision and avoid disappointment. Perhaps you've taken on too much or maybe you're feeling underwhelmed with your position. A symbol of phallic potency, the Ace of Wands, when reversed, might also suggest infertility issues or sexual challenges within a new relationship.

SUMMARY

ACE OF WANDS:

The drive to create something new, sexual potency, and powerful desire. The download of the vast will of nature into the individual to bring something important into existence. Feel the potency of this energy but use it wisely, with respect, or it will overpower you. **Reversed:** Lack of will to move ahead with your ideas. Unfocused and uninspired, insufficient knowledge to achieve what you want. Research things well; know what you want to achieve.

TWO OF WANDS

I DARE TO CLIMB TO NEW HEIGHTS.

This card represents the desire for greater discovery, a willingness to risk life and limb to gain greater perspective, scaling new heights, commanding the best vantage point. This card indicates that you need to gain a greater perspective on a particular project, relationship, or life situation in order to inspire some form of possible resolution and subsequent next steps. It may also indicate that a higher purpose or cause is calling you into action, and you need to find your bearings and plan your move toward it. In the card, the character, identity hidden, is precariously balanced on the pinnacle of an incredibly tall building that he has just scaled with phenomenal agility and athleticism. He clasps the two wands that look set to roar off into the sky. From his towering perch, he can see across a vast distance; below him, a settlement built in some great circle. The two wands he grasps are gathering power and momentum, asserting a rocket force that wants to be released into the space around them and find their destination. He faces a choice—will he allow them to lift him off the summit and propel him somewhere unknown, trusting their guidance, or will he hold on to them and wait until he has a proper fix on the direction he wants them to power him toward? All-seeing eyes, an alien presence has arrived, and he has not yet realised that this higher intelligence is right behind him. One must wonder whether this fleet of UFOs is an emissary carrying

a great promise, or does it pose a threat? They symbolise the astonishing potential of adventure and new horizons that are often present, right here, but go unnoticed, because we are so otherwise preoccupied. The possibility of something truly amazing is as yet unnoticed. He is obviously on a covert mission, not wishing to be recognised, and we can assume he is acting for either self-interest or for a higher cause, where both possibilities involve some risk if he is recognised. And so we revisit that moment of choice, to fly with the force of both wands, ideas that have their own intrinsic energy, or should he hold on and use their energy to plan and execute the next phase of his adventure? The moment of decision, two pathways: to direct with one's own will or be directed by the will of something else. This card suggests that wherever you are in your life, it would be advisable to gain a greater perspective, standing back before the fireworks of inspiration, an incredible idea, seize you and send you flying. Review your position; can you see the landscape ahead, the trajectory of this possibility, or does there need to be much more research before you embark on something new? There is tremendous advantage in taking the time to see and investigate the bigger picture, understanding how the topography of your life—your goals and dreams—spans out across time and space. The possibility is absolutely present for you to reach previously unimaginable heights with your ideas and sense of purpose.

Reversed: Staying on the ground, unwilling to gain fresh perspective or move out of your comfort zone. Unable to really see where you are going, and to plan accordingly. Letting go of opportunities, launching too soon, and unable to direct your gifts. Being distracted and missing crucial information. No plan of action.

Summary

Two of Wands:

The desire to expand one's vision, gaining greater perspective, skill, and wisdom absorbed from distant places and fresh sources. Using the value of opposites to create new ideas that rise above the crowd. Taking considered risks to reach a higher possibility. **Reversed:** Restricted viewpoint and stuck in what you already know. Fuel your imagination; step out of what you already know.

THREE OF WANDS

I EXPAND MY HORIZONS.

The Three of Wands indicates that you are moving ahead with success, confident that you are aligning your skills and talent to achieve something of value—not only for yourself, but for others too. Whether you have set your sights on furthering a career or business that will support yourself and perhaps other dependents, you feel that you are being called by life to manifest something of significance. You sense a growing purposefulness in your character, having clearly understood what is important to you and how you might change some small part of the world in front of you, for the better. In the card artwork, a strong figure stands with his back to us, overlooking a mystical cityscape of jewelled towers and turrets. A wand is held securely in his left hand, an offering or signal. A series of extraordinary tentacled creatures hover before him, emanating energy traces that warp the sky. From the calm, solid countenance of the man, we can assume that these creatures or mystical entities are benevolent and are attracted to him. It's as if they are there to bestow some gift or exchange, and we see that the one drawing close on his left is releasing a shower of gold pieces. He stands in his power, confident and ready to receive the riches and energy they bring because he is clear about the greater purpose this abundance will serve. In his book *Power vs. Force*, the professor David R. Hawkins describes how influential and powerful figures

in the world emanate warmth, sincerity, and openness, treating everyone as an equal and, above all, aware of the responsibilities of their position. That success carries with it the opportunity and obligation to be the very best one can be. He points out that very successful people realise that they are a channel acted through to create success in the outer world, with little anxiety about losing their status and success. This solid confidence came from the knowledge that the source of their success is inside them, a quality of "being" rather than something "out there" that they need to exercise control over. There is a clear distinction to be made: force is something you have to apply to move something, to gain momentum; power, on the other hand, is something that you emanate, that you readily have access to, anywhere. Pushing away versus pulling in. When the factors of power are fully understood, all fear of threat or being diminished by circumstances fades away, and you can move forward. An example of true power is seen in the logic-defying strength of great energy masters practicing qigong. Often small, seemingly fragile people can withstand even the most sustained and violent attack without any need to resist with force, because they are able to channel chi, the flow of energy in the universe, through themselves. This card is calling you to connect with your inner power, that attractor force that draws things toward you and enables you to expand your horizons. Work on crafting a compelling vision for yourself that inspires and empowers you to develop your talents and connections, attracting the people, resources, and opportunities that you deserve.

Reversed: Pushing harder and harder for diminishing returns. Focused too heavily on "doing" rather than "being," quantity not quality. Feeling exhausted and frustrated: nothing ever works. Constantly losing money no matter how hard you work. Your ideas are passed over, leaving you frantically trying to convince people to give you what you need. Instead of fighting the tide of life that is going out, surrender, step back, and step into yourself instead. It is time to reconnect with all of your "selves."

SUMMARY

THREE OF WANDS:

The attractor force for abundant opportunities, anticipating future events and connections in order to make well-informed decisions and commitments. Being in the right place at the right time. **Reversed:** Inability to see ahead and worrying about what may or may not happen. Work on the inner game and seek wise counsel.

FOUR OF WANDS

I ENROLL OTHERS IN THE STRENGTH OF MY VISION.

The Four of Wands is about creating empowering and potentialising relationships, establishing strong physical and emotional foundations upon which to build a life. In the card artwork, a futuristic couple walk hand in hand across a walkway. At their feet we can notice a crack in the structure, which indicates that they are together but there is space in their togetherness. The four wands, representing the four pillars of life—relationship/love, body/physical, purposeful work, and spiritual development—float on either side of the couple. It can be said that your life is as strong as your weakest pillar. Therefore, the ultimate key is to achieve balance. Building the Pillar of Relationships, for example, means that you have people in your life who recognise and perhaps even identify with your talents, gifts, and potential. They help you create the conditions for honesty, acknowledging your strengths and assisting you in seeing and addressing your weaknesses, and giving feedback (as difficult as this can be) in a way that helps you to evolve. The physical pillar is concerned with health, your positive, life-affirming connection to your body, the sacred vessel that carries you through life. It concerns not only the ways you give it nourishment and sustenance, preferably with organic whole foods, but the activities that enliven it and build its healing power and strength. It too addresses the physical environment of your home, which provides the sanctuary

in which to rest, nurture, and reinvigorate yourself with life. The purposeful work pillar is built on shaping and purposefully using your talents and abilities in the cause of something that not only inspires and empowers you but inspires and enlivens others. In return, you are granted the prosperity and resources that will further generate and develop your gifts. The final spiritual pillar is created and built through the knowledge, discipline, and commitment to conscious spiritual practices, such as meditation (of all forms—sitting, moving, walking, mantra chanting, loving kindness, mindfulness), prayer, guided journeying, and the sacred arts. If we become overinvested in one area, the structure becomes unstable. The four pillars can be viewed as the supports of a bridge, which lead from the head or mind to the heart. Love, strength, insight, and light can travel between the head and the heart, creating an open exchange: a unified being. In the artwork, the couple are looking intently at one other, communicating a depth of relationship, commitment, and togetherness. Behind them we see a tall building with a golden flower-of-life geometry rising up the middle, denoting the power of creation and the rich interconnectedness of life. The imposing architectural structure they are walking from tells us that this relationship is backed by the power of something established. We are witnessing a marriage or ceremony of union. Their relationship has been witnessed. This card invites you to look at the structure of your life as a whole. Practically all of us will have pillars or aspects of how we live that are weaker, compromising the integrity of what we wish to build. What pillar of yours needs care and attention? This card points to the possibility of achieving a beautiful balance, steadily working away at each aspect of your life, sharing your experiences with those you love and respect. Enrolling others with the vision you have of yourself inspires them to live theirs.

Reversed: Shaky structure and weak foundations, lack of enrollment and social support, few honest and meaningful connections. Compromised within a relationship, partner not on the same page—mismatch of values, a loss of personal space, always trying to please. Disconnect between head and heart, giving rise to conflicts and miscommunications. Pay attention and do a deep dive into your past history, seeing the connections, the synchronicities, the events, and the people that have given rise to blessed lessons. It is time to balance and refine.

SUMMARY

FOUR OF WANDS:

The strong foundations of partnership, an inner circle rooting for your success, and the resources to build something of strong, lasting value—a legacy. **Reversed:** Shaky foundations, lack of support, and meaningful connections. Build relationships that fully support your highest aspirations.

FIVE OF WANDS

I AM ALERT AND SHARP TO ALL CHALLENGES AND CONFLICTS.

In the Tarot, fives typically represent conflict or disharmony: the dire earth-bound situation in the Five of Pentacles, the watery misery of the Five of Cups, and the tragic, atmospheric conflict of the Five of Swords. At first glance, it would seem that we too are witnessing another tale of destruction with the dramatic conflagration of fighters presented in the Five of Wands. However, we can see no blood, injuries, or death, despite the fiery wands flying like light sabres in all directions. The theatrical, overexaggerated gestures and the strange carnivalesque masks invite us to take a closer look at the action. Tremendous leaps, kicks, and punches and wands thrown as light javelins demonstrate immense physical prowess, athleticism, and skill, a youthful bravado—even celebratory—a display of potential lethality. Ritualised enactments of conflict, mainly between young men, exist in many cultures around the world. For example, on the island of Lombok, Indonesia, armed with long "rattan sticks" and rectangular light wooden shields, the fighters attack each other under the watchful eye of a referee, accompanied by the metallic timbre of traditional Gamelan music. Using a multitude of elaborate gesticulations, often theatrical and comical, they lash out at their opponents with wide-eyed ferocity. As well as its historical associations and popularity at ceremonies, the stick fight, named Peresean, also serves to ask God

for rain for the imminent season of planting, empowering an ancient belief that the more blood that was spilled, the more rain would follow. The use of ritualised forms of antagonistic behaviour, or tests of strength, allows for the integration of our natural aggression. We are introduced to some of the harsh realities of life: the battle and struggle for limited resources or the fierce competition of procreation. Moreover, Mother Nature is appeased by the blood, shed in restitution for man's dishonour, disrespect, and neglect of her—balance is restored. The sacrificial gift of blood, thanking her for her bounteous generosity in supporting the villagers' lives. So too in the animal kingdom, where the strutting, the striking and biting, the flashing of ridiculously grand plumes, and horns or claws allow the battle of dominance to take place as a staged display. Unlike humanity, actual physical fighting to the blood within the same species is rare, because the evolutionary cost is simply too high. This card invites you to consider where you can test your ideas and your mettle: your mental and physical skills in an arena of good will and healthy competition. The ultracompetitive, technologically advanced world we live in also requires that we test and hone our skills before venturing into real-world business ventures or situations where the risk of losing is potentially costly. It is vital to first test our skills in the simulation environments that allow us to learn, grow, and perfect our game. This is an integral part of problem-solving, remaining calm and being adaptive in volatile and unpredictable markets and niches. There is great power in ritual, in acknowledging the fragile balance of life and so honouring your own life and those of your future sparring partners, your competition, which will make you strong.

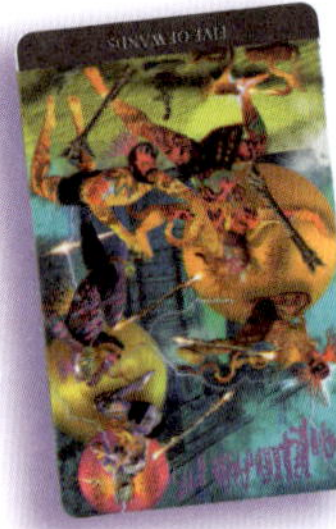

Reversed: Provoking conflict through unskilled communication and clumsy words and actions. When faced with a challenge or potential conflict, unable to powerfully defend your position. Missing the sacred aspect of life, becoming obsessed with winning, hurting others through a lack of empathy and awareness. No sense of real accomplishment; feeling hollow when a desired outcome is achieved.

SUMMARY

FIVE OF WANDS:

Being ready and able to defend your point of view, planned and practiced arguments. Unfazed by opposition yet able to listen and take stock of what may not work. **Reversed:** Lack of skills to support your plans, creating unnecessary conflict, blaming others. Acknowledging failure and using it to learn and grow.

SIX OF WANDS

I LEAD THROUGH EXAMPLE.

This is a card of success, a celebration of a well-chosen goal or ambition. A perfect opportunity to celebrate what you have already achieved, knowing that you have rightly earned this success. There is no hesitation, no sense of being a fraud; you have proved yourself beyond capable and have mustered everyone's approval. In the card artwork, we see the ritualised return of a great hero: part homage to artist Jack Burnley's original 1940s Starman superhero, part Renaissance statue. His return sparks both adulation and fear at the formidable powers and knowledge he has acquired from the distant lands conquered. The return of such a hero will also provoke resentment amongst those less worthy who had ruled in his absence. Not all the bows he receives are a mark of respect. Like the great hero Odysseus in Homer's epic poem the *Odyssey*, this returning leader may well have much treachery to deal with at home. To leave one's home and venture off, no matter how noble the cause, means this aspect of life is left to the wanderings of fate. In this, the one who returns in triumph must be alert to their immediate environment. As the hero in the artwork, to display your power can act as a warning to those who would be quick to undermine you. It will not stop them, however, but will allow time to access the dynamics wisely. Along with the possible threats, there is also space for a wondrous celebration. To venture forth and accomplish

something of intense difficulty must be fully acknowledged. It is also the time to move out and shine with new ideas. While you may have self-belief in the rightness of your offering to the world, it must be understood that success can be extremely fleeting. In order to really engineer and carry success for some time in the future, you must enroll others in the value of your mission. You need to elicit their value system and create a cohesive strategy that will align their needs and ambitions with your own. Acting not merely as a figurehead but really embarking on the task of true leadership—of clearly defining a vision that is in everyone's best interests. The ultimate win-win situation that is unifying, supportive, and gratifying for all involved. This card therefore suggests that you are being invited to step forward into a position of leadership in your work or social life. Good leadership is always about moving toward a shared vision that preferably symbolises the most promising of human virtues. Great leaders create an exciting, energising, and optimistic environment, coaching and affirming their teammates while being honest, accountable, compassionate, and ultimately decisive. They are not afraid to take the brunt of criticism and are able to offer encouraging feedback, fine-tuning a pathway to success. It is time to invest in your own leadership abilities and be inspired and learn from leaders around you, investigating ways that you can now take the lead—inspire.

Reversed: This card suggests that there is the danger that recent success might be only fleeting. Having put so much of yourself into this project or goal, it is important to maintain momentum. While it is tempting to put your feet up and pat yourself on the back, resist. It is grace that all the elements have come together to act in your favour. Everything is about timing. You may be the flavour of the month, but you must capitalise on your visibility, maintain humility, and acknowledge the roles and efforts of the other players that are instrumental to your success.

SUMMARY

SIX OF WANDS:

The return of the hero who has risked everything for a greater cause, highly influential, offering the possibility of what the human spirit is capable of achieving. Time to acknowledge your gifts and your experience and to build upon them. **Reversed:** Inability to command respect, weak leadership and commitment. Make your words mean something; do what you say.

SEVEN OF WANDS

I WILL NOT GIVE IN/UP.

The Seven of Wands indicates a struggle to maintain a position. From an initial stance of success, there will be challenges from others fighting to achieve the same results. When something is worth having, the competition is fierce, and we must continually prove ourselves and call upon every ounce of power and skill in order to triumph. If your vision and creative effort are fully realised, attracting acclaim, then you must expect competition and challenge. Other people and organisations will also desire the same benefits and recognition as you, and be prepared to act decisively to get them. In the card we see the character of a warrior hero artfully perched on the edge of a concrete block ravaged by war. Chaos and destruction rain down on him, but he is poised and ready to defend his position. Although the assault is merciless and assassins stalk him on the ground, there is no sense that he is defeated. There is even a wry smile on his face, indicating that he is free even in the throes of the maelstrom. He knows that freedom arises when there is nowhere else to go and nothing else to do except what you are doing: the decisive moment is upon him. In the sky a vulture hovers, awaiting a fresh cadaver to pick clean, but it will not be his. While it appears that the way forward is blocked and your vision is in danger of being destroyed, you must call upon your talents, self-belief, and sheer determination to withstand the challenges and obstacles. It is vital to remember that when you masterfully create and live a truly powerful vision, it too has "intelligence" that can guide and keep you focused when

the going gets tough. It is time to see just how formidable and tenacious you are when you believe in something, when you take a stand for something important. Most of my adult life has been about bringing creative ideas to life, and I can say wholeheartedly that this card of fierce opposition will come into your arena at some point. If you have been an innovator or challenged something in a particularly ingenious way, you will come up against criticism and hostility. There will be times when severe challenges will fly at you from all angles. Intense resistance can also surface as you get close to completing a project that carries great potential: the closer you get, the bigger the dragons. This is why so many extraordinary ideas never actually make it off the launchpad, or they end up watered down and compromised. The German philosopher Arthur Schopenhauer is often credited as saying that truth passes through three stages: first, it is ridiculed; second, it is violently opposed; third, it is accepted as self-evident. Often the same pattern awaits a great creative idea. Working with Bowie, the guiding principle was always that creativity would never, under any circumstances, be compromised. Creating the artwork for the *Outside* album, I found myself dealing with worried publicity departments on several occasions, wanting to remove a particularly provocative element from the art. In every case, Bowie would wave the opposition aside; originality must triumph. There was never any question of doing something to be popular or to please people. In this spirit, it is time to strengthen your resolve. If you have a strong enough "Why," the "How" will be taken care of. The ability to defend a vision against tremendous objection and setbacks is key to following through, not letting anything derail the cause. There is genius in not giving up.

Reversed: So many people spend their precious life force fighting for things that are not worth fighting for: time, energy, and resources frittered away on petty disputes, the small stuff of life. Additionally, they may battle against the odds with true strength and passion, only to discover it was for a misguided cause. Grandiosity lavished on ill-conceived ideas and impressive claims, and yet nothing of real substance to back them up. It may be pertinent to go back to your drawing board and take a good, hard look at what you are trying to achieve and why—what are you trying to prove about yourself and life?

SUMMARY

SEVEN OF WANDS:

The ability to defend a vision against tremendous opposition and setbacks is key to meaningful success, not letting anything derail the cause. There is genius in not giving up, even when surrounded by doubters and fierce competition. **Reversed:** Fighting for the wrong cause, unwillingness to clearly see and be moved by injustice or unfairness. Check your vision and motives: What are you truly willing to put your heart and soul into?

EIGHT OF WANDS

I CAN MAKE THIS HAPPEN.

The Eight of Wands shifts from the intense fiery struggles of the Seven of Wands to the magical glow of visions heading for the stars. A sense of the mystical has replaced the antagonism, and we can now see the light emanating from a luminous destination. The Eight of Wands contains a high level of energy and thrust that propels ideas and adventures forward. As ideas soar high, though, there is still much work to be taken care of. This is no time to just sit and gaze at the sky, because this card demands very focused attention. Eights deal with structure—the geometries—while the Wands carry the raw combustion energy. Raw energy without a structure becomes rogue energy, unable to be harnessed toward a goal or purpose. Once you have the accurate geometry of your trajectory and the propellant to reach where you want to go, you can work with complete concentration—your productivity increases exponentially. However, there is almost always a natural tendency to relax into the ride when things start to move decisively toward a destination. Yet, in this instance, you must remain focused on the important details. It is in the supreme detailing of a product, an invention, a work of art or piece of music—separating the wheat from the chaff—that is the difference that makes all the difference. The elements of an idea can arrive rapier fast, but it is in the details, the unique composition and interplay of the elements, that a

good idea is separated from a really outstanding idea. Very often, though, the detailing can be exacting and agonising: being willing to draw or compose something for the tenth time when the ninth was good enough, or to minutely adjust the bass on a track in an all-night stint to get it as good as it possibly can be. This is the part where the final boost to get into outer orbit can sometimes empty the fuel tanks, and we must hope that we have gained just enough propulsion to reach the frictionless vacuum of space. Greatness demands a drive unseen in most people. As you work on an idea, what would raise it just that fraction more to transform it from good to exceptional? Hard work isn't enough to achieve success. You must always be learning, with the aim to continually improve. You must be discerning and humble enough to understand what is working and what isn't, and to act on what you discover. You must become skilled at creating the environmental conditions that make success inevitable.

Reversed: Unable to launch. Lack of energy, discipline, and drive. Unable or unwilling to listen and pay attention to feedback and to be able to adjust course along the way. Fragmented focus, playing safe, settling for second best. Examine the systems, structures, and resources you have in place to see what's missing or can be improved. Meditate and pray for guidance from your own internal navigation system.

SUMMARY

EIGHT OF WANDS:

Gather the resources and energy required to propel you forward. Actively engage in realising your most-creative and most-powerful ideas. Taking off in your career and in your personal life. Soaring to new heights. **Reversed:** Unable to launch. Lack of energy and enthusiasm, fragmented focus, playing safe. Revitalise your vision, think big, and take consistent action.

NINE OF WANDS

I AM WILLING TO FACE THE DARKNESS AND NEGATIVITY.

This card expresses the courage, self-reliance, and vitality required to manage the pain and weariness endured in the ongoing battle with ignorance, judgment, and hostility. Our own and everybody else's. It speaks of the fortitude required—mental, physical, and spiritual—to see things through when others would abandon hope and give up. The Nine of Wands shows a powerful street fighter in the throes of tackling something dark and foreboding. Throughout history, religions, legends, and belief systems have described how shadowy supernatural entities emerge out of the darkness to interfere and ruin our lives. Ultimately, though, these myths are describing how the real battle to unleash our true creative spirit takes place in the mind. It is in the realm of the mind that we must face the supreme challenge: the internal voice, seemingly our own voice, that shapes our destiny. In the dark recesses of our imagination lurks the one that we must do battle with in order to live fully expressed. Our unconscious fears and trepidations are visualised in the art as a jet-black rip in the fabric of reality, out of which a menacing, mechanised hand reaches forth to propel a bolt of dark, malevolent energy. We see three gold teeth representing the possibility of freedom from the enslavement of the mind. Back in time, when a man bought his own freedom he would display his freedom and his newfound "wealth" by showing how many gold teeth he could afford. Rendering a connection with the Devil card, we once again notice the

emerald crystal, connecting to the emerald tablet, denoting that this card is another gateway to the secret of the *prima materia*, the first matter, chaos, space, the dark womb that births life. Rather than the possibility of this secret wonder, which is beyond duality, falling into the hands of the Devil, here it conveys the potential of freedom from that possible fate. As described in Martin Ruland the Younger's 1612 alchemical dictionary, the *prima materia* comprises all colours and, potentially, all metals; there is nothing more glorious in the world, for it induces itself and gives birth to itself. As in the works of alchemy, we too contain the potential for every colour, every sound, every form, touch, feeling, sensation, and beyond. We too carry the same directive: to give birth to ourselves. Therefore, this card expresses a sign of hope, offering the possibility of being free of the most corrosive and debilitating force that stops us achieving our full potential: the hidden shadow within our minds. Not only the personal shadow, of course, but the world or human shadow; the treachery, torture, and violence of the collective unconscious that in the past was projected onto gods and the movement of the stars. No army can equal the destructive force of the collective human shadow. This immense shadow, that of the transpersonal, manipulates and sculpts our lesser personal shadows, mixing our own unique misgivings, sorrows, and fears with its own, gathered from the dawn of mankind. We carry an inherited database and response to the burden of existence, spirit manifest in form. This card invites you to seek your own freedom from the shadow interloper by shining the light of awareness. Witness the voice in your head; know that it isn't yours but is transmitted to you in the act of conception/birth. Life is the journeying into the world to uncover this voice, making it conscious, so that at last the pain and restriction it causes can be dissolved: recognising its falseness, tracing its origins, and then, with the grace of love, releasing and cleansing yourself of it. Each moment holds that potential.

Reversed: Being trapped in the prison of negative thoughts. A real sense of limitation and defeat. Attracting conflict, making enemies, feeling offended, under attack. Retreat and take great care. Lick your wounds and explore ways to move and release this negative energy. Journal, draw, paint, sculpt—express the negativity so it can be clearly seen, faced, and released. Create a meaningful ritual to burn away the negative representation; repeat if you need to. Choose uplifting, affirming, and inspiring talks, podcasts, images, and music to recharge. Be kind and gentle with yourself.

SUMMARY

NINE OF WANDS:

The pain and weariness endured in the ongoing battle with ignorance, judgment, and inequality. Relentlessly seeing things through, keeping the vision alive when others would abandon hope. **Reversed:** Attracting conflict, making enemies, feeling offended, under attack. Don't take things personally, master your emotions, act with wisdom, and desire for only the highest outcome.

TEN OF WANDS

I CARRY THE BURDENS OF LIFE WHILE MARVELLING AT THE SMALL MIRACLES.

The tens in Tarot represent the completion of intense cycles, fraught with danger, psychologically complex, impregnated with possibilities. This card determines that you have arrived at the climax of an epic odyssey. In overcoming the negative force of the mind's shadows in the Nine of Wands, you have tenaciously given life to a creative venture, realised a dream, or accomplished a major goal. And yet, as you reach the summit of this metaphorical mountain, you face possibly an even-bigger challenge ahead. You must now deal with the consequences of success and achievement. A path that is mirrored in so many mythological adventures; where the intrepid hero arrives at the promised land, battered and bruised, only to discover that this is in fact where the real work begins. We are led to believe that there is some place to reach, where suddenly everything will be just fine and all our problems will vanish, the fairy-tale ending, a Shangri-La. That if we work hard enough, smart enough, we too can save up to build our own paradise. Overwhelming evidence suggests otherwise—we only have to look at the dysfunctional and often-destructive lives of countless celebrities and high achievers. We somehow believe in the formula of When . . . then . . . , as in *When* I have this, *then* I'll be happy, or when I do this, then I'll be happy and content, the never-ending list. The very essence of life is movement; change is the only constant. There is no continuous realm of happiness. No matter what we may achieve, life will

move on, and we must still deal with the realities of our human existence. If we can accept that life is an ever-shifting landscape, we will cease to crave the highs and curse the lows. If we understand that anything worth achieving, even great achievements, is simply stations on the journey back into the open arms of providence, then we will not be shattered by what lies ahead. We travel STATION to STATION. The happy ever after, it turns out, is the moment we find ourselves in right now. In the artwork we see the ancient Mother Tree hovering above a graffiti-strewn wall of steps. This symbolises the effort it takes to achieve something, to reach a goal. All the twisted wands of the *Starman Tarot* are gifted from the ancient Mother Tree. Throughout this suit, the wands flow between different roles: a flaming torch of hope; a lethal, flaming weapon; an attractor for abundance or a symbol of togetherness and stability. In this card they take on the role of the burdens we must carry. As we look past the stooped figure, the steps that lead nowhere are repeated into the distance, under the watchful gaze of the giant Starman statues. The animal skeletons that move across the sands suggest that time will erode everything, and the star-decorated scorpion, the sting of life, skulks behind us. Bending to pick up the wand, this battered soul sees the astonishing beauty of a fresh rose growing up through the chain links on the ground, and his hand impulsively reaches for it. The rose offers a moment of wonder and beauty. Moments filled with sadness and others with joy. This card invites you to cherish such moments of beauty and wonderment, precious and delicate as a flower growing in the desert. Put down your burdens for a moment and just marvel in the miracle of it all. Life is made up of small moments; we must carry on what needs to be done, for the Mother Tree has work for us to do.

Reversed: Being the victim or martyr, the "poor me," unwilling to face the weakness of never giving your best, always blaming others for your misfortune, never taking responsibility. The inability to actually make a difference and touch the lives of others. Everything is conditional: it's all about ME. It may be prudent to investigate the origins of your "victim" story, normally acquired through some profound childhood wounding. Great or small, it needs to be attended to; seen for what it is and released through, for example, breathwork, hypnotherapy, or meditation. Ask for guidance; weed out the negativity. Forgive yourself.

SUMMARY

TEN OF WANDS:

The demands of life can feel overbearing. You may be feeling abused and exploited, overwhelmed and unable to cope, unsupported, resigned to living life as a complaint. Instead, actively seek out the wins, the moments of goodness, to regain strength gain sight of a higher possibility. **Reversed:** Stuck in the past, playing the victim. Forgive yourself and others; let go of the past. Refocus on what you can change and are willing to do.

ACE OF SWORDS

I LIVE THROUGH MY HIGHEST VALUES.

The time has arrived for a significant breakthrough—the creation of conscious intentional space in which to have a powerful insight. Conscious understanding brought to a particular issue is expanded with a clear, unique thought or new inner voice. The result is rejuvenating, a fresh new beginning or approach to life, with a renewed vision of your purpose. In the artwork the sword is seen floating in the space of pure, geometric potential, enveloped by the light colour spectrum, where all human visions are birthed into reality, the alchemy of a quest potentialised. Its ancient Celtic blade, weathered by time and circumstance, points upward past the clouds of doubt to the new heights that beckon you. The sword, which represents intelligence, appears to sever the umbilical cord that joins the airy fetuses floating toward future possibilities. The male and female ancestral lines of struggle, hardship, and limited being in the world are being severed. A great liberation is catalysed. This card calls upon you to cut away all that is not moving you toward your highest potential and service in the world. It invites the birth

and collaboration of all your intelligences so that you can live into the full force field of your life. Advanced brain-mapping technologies can visually illustrate the different types of intelligence, overturning the long-held notion of innate preferences—left- vs. right-brain intelligence. The theory of multiple intelligences as opposed to unified general intelligence, IQ, for instance, aims to broaden the definition so that it reflects the many ways that people think, learn, and act. For example, the agility, skill, strength, and precision of a modern dancer may be said to have a combination of bodily kinaesthetic and visual spatial intelligences, while someone such as Bowie would be said to have a predominant musical-rhythmic and harmonic intelligence—an acute sensitivity to musical components and pitch, combined with a high verbal-linguistic intelligence and existential intelligence, which was expressed through his striking lyrics, which plucked the creative heart of so many people throughout his long career. This card indicates an opportunity for powerful focus, gathering and honing all your intelligences in the spirit of great teamwork, to work toward a vision of yourself realising your highest potential, flow, and radiance. Consider fresh ways of understanding, organising, articulating, and expressing your sense of purpose. You can achieve anything you desire.

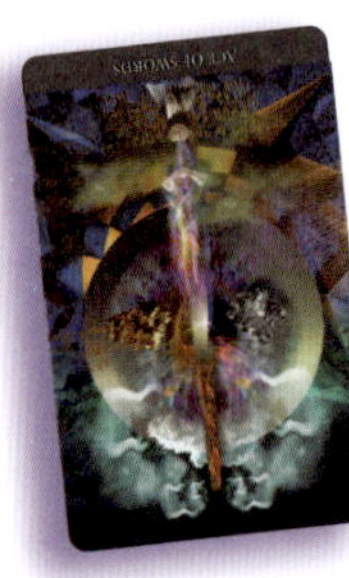

Reversed: There is holding on to the past, a refusal to move forward, rigidity and unwillingness to change, experiment, and explore. Nothing new can arise. A lack of confidence in your intelligence and capabilities causes tremendous inertia. It is time for a deep dive, to methodically expose yourself to past successes, triumphs, and lessons learned, drawing on your own memories and those of dear friends, family members, and associates. Turn up the light of awareness and "witness" your self-talk. Meet negative thoughts with their exact opposite, a positive affirmation, and begin a practise of daily gratitude.

SUMMARY

ACE OF SWORDS:

The power of the mind to cut away what's irrelevant in order to shape your true destiny. Embodying a powerful philosophy, letting go of limited and outdated ancestral patterns, whist also honouring and using the wisdom of what has gone before. **Reversed:** Holding on to the past, rigidity, unwillingness to change. Experiment, explore, and embrace new ideas.

TWO OF SWORDS

I TRUST MY ABILITY TO FIND MY WAY.

This card speaks about choice. It asks us to consider what it means to make a powerful choice—what it actually involves. We can consider a distinction between a choice and a decision; they are often viewed as two words with the same meaning. A decision is about looking backward, weighing up the past, and moving forward on the basis of what we conclude. A choice, on the other hand, is completely free of the past, arising out of a clear open awareness, space, nothing. There are no reasons or justifications in a choice; it is simply made. Decisions therefore exist in the domain of the small, egoic self, attached to its stories about life, while choices arise spontaneously out of the freedom of the universal self. We gift ourselves choice but must work and deliberate when making a decision. Importantly, both ways have value when used wisely. In our culture, we appear to have greater and greater choices, but if we look closely, it becomes clear that what we actually have are more and more options arising within the same limited context. This is far from giving us freedom, and we are overwhelmed with alternatives that require us to sift through more and more information to make a decision. To go one way or another becomes an agonising cloud of information. There are times when we need to reference the past and gain some additional knowledge; the key is to recognise when we are getting lost in all the detail. Don Juan Matus, the

Mexican shaman, characterised by Carlos Castaneda, asked a simple yet profound question when faced with two different paths: "Does this path have a heart?" He goes on to state that all paths are the same: they lead nowhere. Like Don Juan, I would say that a path with no heart is devoid of joy, with no sense of expansion; even to take it feels intensely difficult. However, over time, like so many discomforts and situations we tolerate, the way of least joy becomes normalised. For me, a path with heart isn't automatically easy; it can present incredible challenges and it carves out the vessel of emotion, making it deeper, and yet, it feels expansive, exciting, and evolutionary. In the artwork we see the woman at the bottom of the steps, quite literally split between two possible paths behind her, and yet, she appears calm and balanced. Her light of intelligence shines from within. The two paths look similar but present her with different possibilities: Which way should she go? The wolf symbolises a deep connection with intuition—inner-tuition. There is no obvious right way to go. This is the point of choice. This is your point of power.

Reversed: Stuck in endless options, unable to evoke the power of choice. Fear of getting it wrong. Making the same mistakes over and over again. Drifting through life without any meaningful direction and giving your power away to others. You must rewrite your relationship with failure, and in the words of Samuel Beckett, "Ever tried. Ever failed. No matter. Try again. Fail again. Fail better." Implying that every time we choose and fail, we learn something more about ourselves and life; every failure ultimately contains the seed of success.

SUMMARY

TWO OF SWORDS:

The pressure to make an important choice is handled by not rushing and trusting your instincts and inner wisdom; make a choice when you are ready, not when others say so. The journey is more important than the destination, so choose a path with heart. **Reversed:** Unwilling and afraid to choose, stuck, fear of risking failure. Make a choice, and if it doesn't work out, take the learning and choose again.

THREE OF SWORDS

I VIEW LIFE AS CRUEL AND MEANINGLESS.

Seeing a world that appears to be so cruel and uncompromising can bring us to a point of despair. In the artwork the young man sits with his head down, and we can feel his sense of deep sadness. I imagined him as a street artist, expressing his anguish through his art; behind him, on the wall, is his creation. The head of the floating surreal figure is a "mask of shame," a medieval torture device worn for the purpose of public humiliation and rejection. Throughout history, people have been forced to display a mark of shame, a stigma to deter others. This taps into something very primal. In early humans, where survival was intimately linked with collaboration, to be rejected by your tribe was effectively a death sentence. In later cultures, artists, writers, and intellectuals—anyone who dared to think differently or admit a different sexual orientation—risked being shamed and outcast. The violence and suffering that human beings can inflict on other humans and, indeed, all living creatures is utterly overwhelming. And yet, it exists and cannot be ignored. Three swords are propped up against the wall, one of them almost falling against the sitting figure, as if they have been carelessly left behind by their owners. As objects, they are crafted pieces of metal just sitting against the wall, but in the hands of men, they can cause unimaginable suffering. The hawk and the feather tell us that even in the face of despair, there sits the possibility

of freedom and greater vision. The dripping heart—painted almost as an afterthought—communicates that only through love, the heart, can we be liberated from the burdens of existence. The luminous fetus offers hope of rebirth that awaits within the darkest depths, the fullness of being that can be reached only when we are able to touch our deepest sorrow. The question mark sign, roughly painted, gives us a clue as to how we can transform our reality. This card suggests that the quality of your life experience is directly proportional to the quality of the questions that you ask. And so another interpretation of the figure emerges, as one who, like the Buddha, sits determined to penetrate the truth. He will not move from his spot until he has an answer. Many spiritual teachings describe how we must go down through layer after layer of our personality until we get to the last layer and fall through into a space that is meaningless and empty. But if we are able to fall yet further into the darkness of meaninglessness, we arrive at "nothing." From nothing we can create anything. This card tells us that our sorrow must be acknowledged; the despair is something we all share. When we see that it carries the seeds of new growth, we can surrender to it, allowing it to move through and transform us.

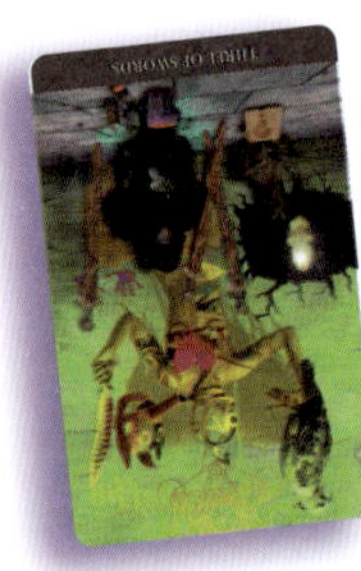

Reversed: Constantly trying to stay positive, putting on a brave face despite feeling despair. Avoiding anything potentially sad or emotionally difficult and not expressing your truth. Becoming cold, cut off, and inflicting misery on self and others. Acknowledge rather than hide your despair and seek out fellowship. Know that everyone reaches despair; however, a problem shared is a problem halved. When we express our hopelessness with those who have faced similar hardships, we gain not only companionship, but empathy and understanding for the suffering of others.

SUMMARY

THREE OF SWORDS:

The sorrow and existential misery of the human condition can seem incomprehensible. The quiet desperation, broken hearts, physical and psychological suffering, and pain appear ubiquitous. But we must not lose sight of the immense good, the astonishing acts of kindness alongside the small, meaningful generosities that happen all around. **Reversed:** Falsely staying positive, denying the shadow. Discover the power of surrender, handing your life over to a power greater than self. Diving fully into emotions, transforming through creative self-expression.

FOUR OF SWORDS
I ALLOW MYSELF TO REST IN STILLNESS.

A time of rest and recuperation is needed after challenges and difficulty; a chance to recharge. Allow yourself a period of contemplation and stillness, rejuvenating the mind and body. To sit in stillness and not do anything presents a different challenge as we observe the incessant mental chatter, but slowly we can see it as just the activity of an overactive mind. When we focus on the breath and the accompanying bodily sensations, we can come into the present moment. In the present we are simply aware of what is arising, unburdened by thoughts pertaining to the past or the future. In meditation and stillness, we dissolve the illusion of ego to reveal the gift, the Golden Eternity, as described by Jack Kerouac in his book *The Scripture of the Golden Eternity*, which conveys the Mystic's sense of rest and unity in all things. Cultivating the art of presence is our greatest gateway to true happiness. The card depicts the Starman sitting in meditation, holding two swords by the blades. The implements of action and violence are transformed into tools of meditation, delicately balanced on his knees. In front of him there spins a gyroscope; he will not remain sitting for longer than it naturally spins. This time of rest is strategic, an integral part of a well-balanced, multifaceted life. The diamond geometry pattern emanating from his third eye refers to the Diamond Sutra, the discourse of the Buddha on the nature of ultimate reality. MRI scans have

revealed that the brain's "fight or flight" centre, the amygdala, the primal region of the brain associated with fear and emotion, actually shrinks in size when people meditate and practise mindfulness. In contrast, neuroplasticity, your brain's ability to change, adapt, and learn, is greatly impaired by stress and burnout, and most other organs of the body are adversely affected too. Chronic stress, the physiological or psychological response induced by an internal (recollected) or external stressor lasting for weeks and months, is a killer. It is crucial to have a period of rest and replenishment after a time of intense work or any form of trauma. This card then suggests that it is time for you to take a break from the persistent activity and thrust of life, to investigate the nature of the mind through the powerful process of breath and observation. As we at times are forced to take care of the body, this is your time to support, nourish, and cleanse the mind, giving yourself space. Life is relentless, with the stories of our lives revealing themselves moment to moment; however, there are times when you must simply stop. Like the space between words that gives form to sentences, being still is as important as taking action.

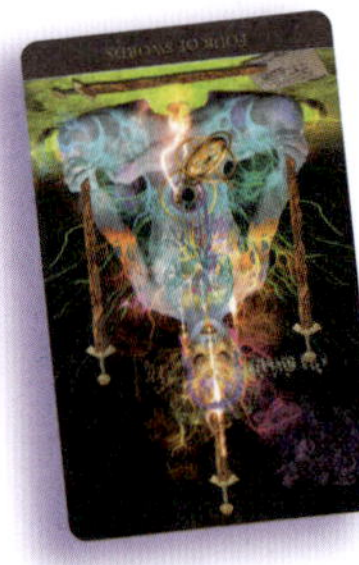

Reversed: Constantly busy, must be doing something to prove that you have value. Racing mind causing both inner and outer confusion, conflict, and overwhelmingness. Chronic stress leading to physical and mental fatigue and burnout. No time to connect with the people and things that really matter. This is a strong signal to refocus; to get out of your head and into your body. Plan and prepare nourishing meals, walk in nature, exercise, have bodywork, do breathwork, or receive deep-tissue massage and reflexology to realign.

Summary

Four of Swords:

The fullness of stillness, a sacred space that is replenishing and rejuvenating, birthing renewal. Patient exploration of inner realms and dreams, receiving answers. No need to rush into things. The alchemy of transforming negativity into the energy that fuels new ideas and potentials. **Reversed:** Too much movement, overactive mind, confusion and overwhelmingness. Ground yourself in a nourishing, daily practice; touch the earth with your feet and hands.

FIVE OF SWORDS

I MUST WIN AT ANY COST.

Winning of any kind will always involve sacrifices, and at first glance, the difference between "winning at a cost" and at "any cost" might seem trivial, but deeper inspection uncovers the stories of lives and careers brazenly sacrificed, shattered, and broken. In the conflagration of a blinding obsession and quest for power and control, people cease to be people, instead becoming objects or instruments that merely help or hinder progress. Colleagues become competitors; family and friends, dead weight. The ancient Roman orator Marcus Tullius Cicero is quoted as saying "*Inter arma enim silent leges*," often misused, "In times of war, the law falls silent," which, even today, leaders with a relentless drive to succeed have used to justify their immoral actions. Ignore laws to get what you want; conquer at all costs. This demonstrates the dangerous manipulation of words taken out of context. The art depicts a man, sword in hand, poised to strike. Below him, a man kneels surrendered, apparently injured, draining of life force. It is set in a cold, uncompromising land, the remains of death littering the landscape signifying the physical and emotional carnage that follows in the wake of those prepared to sacrifice anything to achieve their goal. In a flash of brilliance, the radiant hand of John the Baptist, said to have baptised Jesus, appears—as if to awaken the aggressor from a trance. He stands composed, ready to strike the blow that will secure victory.

The scene is frozen in time, posing the question of what will happen next—will the sword fall or will this man be spared? Within the pause . . . that instant . . . another possibility can be born. The drive and determination to succeed in an endeavour are admirable; the aspiration to positively influence and have maximum impact in one's community and farther afield is exemplary—but not if you leave a trail of destruction. This card represents the galvanising force of ambition, of striding toward a goal. It requests that you look carefully at where you may be fixated on an outcome and acting out of integrity. For instance, you may want to look at the ways you are being self-righteous, placing the need to be right over and above loving and respectful connection. The compulsion to win, to always be right, cuts away at the heart of life, and we are asked to consider whether it's worth the sacrifice. There is always a pregnant pause available where we are presented with the opportunity to take a different action. The realisation is that when you lose sight of what you know is right, you become the victim, unaware you are being driven by forces that will lead you to the realm of regret and an empty victory.

Reversed: Unable or unwilling to heed the signs that life gives you. Becoming blind to the consequences of your words and actions. Simply pushing too hard. Step back from the project of your life and the apparent virtuosity of your endeavours; gain perspective. Take time to sense the currents of life pulsing around you, and actively appreciate the living vista. Quieten the myriad of voices, the different parts of you that are so eager for action; ask them to stop and instead call upon on the wisdom and practise of gratitude for all of life.

SUMMARY

FIVE OF SWORDS:

The fixation on an outcome, leaving behind a trail of wreckage and upset. Inappropriate use of position and power, ignoring your heart for temporary gain and greed. Waking up to the consequences of selfish actions and harsh words to those we love and people we respect. Taking stock before it's too late. **Reversed:** Unwilling to stop even when it is clear that something is wrong. Constantly pushing until complete burnout. Step back, gain perspective, and put right any harm that's been done.

SIX OF SWORDS

I ADVENTURE INTO THE GREAT UNKNOWN.

So much of our lives are spent trying to avoid change, because to move away from what is familiar involves risk, even danger, and yet, remaining where we are is not easy either. As philosopher Joseph Campbell wrote, "We must let go of the life we have planned, so as to accept the one that is waiting for us." This card indicates that it is time to venture across the unknown sea; something is awaiting your arrival. The card depicts a young tribal warrior sailing his kayak on the great river of life, richly golden with possibility. He has left his home, a journey has called him, and he is willing to face potential dangers in the search for meaning and answers. He balances precariously, perched at the mouth of a waterfall connecting to the vision before him, a spirit guide that breathes new life into his being. To his right, shards of glowing rock, above which an angelic patterning hovers, messengers from a new land. Inertia, a tendency to do nothing or to remain unchanged, often sits at the helm of any changes that we want to make in our lives. As well as our hardwired biology trying to protect us from risk, another ally of inertia is the false impression that we need to feel good or positive about a change in order to move ahead. In fact, very often we are pushed by the sheer force of life circumstance. Many of the greatest works of art and literature have been sparked by the fire of turmoil or birthed from the dark womb of sadness. As I worked

on several of the cards, I felt nothing short of dreadful: existential sadness, feeling completely artistically blocked and even physically ill, and yet, those cards are among the most innovative and profound for me. They turned out to be powerful transition points propelling me to more-vivid creative territories and helping me ask deeper, richer questions. This card communicates the energy of transition; you are being asked to leave behind what is familiar. Transitions are uncomfortable, letting go of what is safe and predictable; suddenly we are flung into a period of chaos where our old knowledge is useless and we must face great uncertainty. The thought of having to start again is scary, terrifying even; however, negotiating the rapids, aware that this is implicit to the journey, we then sail into a neutral or dead zone, where nothing appears to be happening. Deep under the surface of these waters, though, new life is swimming, ready to surface. This card reminds you that the whole of your life is a process, an unending series of transitions and being aware of the cycle: ending/chaos/neutral/beginning can enable us to see it is natural, magical, and extraordinary. A new phase of life.

Reversed: Trying to leap straight into a new phase of life without the conscious work of gleaning insight or wisdom in the process. Remaining stuck in an uncomfortable place; inertia winning. Clinging to outmoded, unhelpful, and false beliefs, going around in circles. Constantly needing to be rescued. It is suggested that you revisit any unfinished business that is hanging around, clouding your judgment and abilities. Open your mind and heart to some satisfactory resolution, clearing the past before you journey forward.

SUMMARY

SIX OF SWORDS:

The innate curiosity and desire to explore, discover, and expand horizons. The drive to experience difference, testing your abilities to gain self-knowledge, being willing to take risks. Not settling for the conventional paths, being open to not knowing. **Reversed:** Setting forth ill-prepared, lacking skill and direction, needing to be rescued. Poorly conceived actions that lead right back to where you started. Clear unfinished business; make sure your information is current and relevant before moving ahead.

SEVEN OF SWORDS

I WANT WHAT OTHERS HAVE.

Deception is at play, betrayal, and also cunning. Ironically, often when we do something in secret, taking special care not to be discovered, a logic-defying energy plays with us: two people speaking who would never normally speak, an email sent to the wrong person, a phone accidentally left face up on a table. Apparently random collisions like this defy all the odds and expose our deceptions. The use of deviousness to gain an advantage or deceive always contains the seeds of its perpetrator's downfall. Most forms of private and public wrongdoings, acts of adultery and other personal betrayals, financial fraud, government corruption—even murder and genocide—are fuelled by lies. Ultimately every lie we tell haunts our future and sours our past. There is no telling when or how it might collide with reality, requiring further maintenance; yet more lies. Conversely, the truth never needs to be tended. In the artwork we see a figure making a dramatic escape, carrying two swords that he has seized from the obscure, floating tank, seemingly a repository guarded by strange disk eye security. The image is a playful reference to the artists Damien Hirst and Jeff Koons, with their talent for reconfiguring things of little perceived value into rare objects. Are the swords artefacts, worthless rusty metal, or fine art? This brings into question just what is value, what makes something intrinsically valuable, who decides? Is the value our culture places

on things in itself a grand deception? The ubiquitous game of restricting supply so that an item is perceived as rare, unique, and precious. Our prevalent communication delivery system, the media, is dripping with stories about the rich and famous, designed to make us drool over lifestyles that are manufactured and empty. Beneath the luxurious, sensual comfort of privilege are the same challenges of love, approval, loss, abandonment, pain, and emptiness we all face. We are bewitched to fill our own longing for wholeness, certainty, and completion with that which is "other." This card asks you to consider those parts of your life where there may be dishonesty and deception. Perhaps you feel that you don't have the time, courage, and energy to meet something head on, instead preferring to avoid it, but this too can become an ingrained pattern that, instead of liberating you, keeps you trapped in a false belief based on fear. Ask yourself where you are not being honest with others and ultimately with yourself. There is an opportunity in this card to put things right and restore your integrity. Wielding your sword, cut away your own lies and mistruths and challenge, with heart and compassion, those in the relationships and culture around you.

Reversed: Courage to expose dishonesty and deception regardless of the personal risk involved to status and reputation. Using ingenuity, cunning, and deception to overcome repression and threatened violence. Hiding the truth to protect the innocent. While it is utterly admirable to protect a principle or people from harm, does it justify the continued use of lies? Might there be another path or way forward where the light of truth can finally be revealed without putting everything in jeopardy, remembering that secrets enclose the healing that can otherwise be released; the seed of light in the darkness, the seed of darkness in the light. Healing; wholeness carries all of it.

Summary

Seven of Swords:

Seeing clearly that all the energy and intelligence it takes to deceive and steal, sometimes risking reputation, honour, and even life, can instead be used to create lasting and meaningful outcomes for everyone. We must stay aware that trust and integrity are sacred, not to be sacrificed for the sake of personal gain and power. Understanding that we all carry the burden of secrets filled with fear and shame, and having compassion. **Reversed:** Unwilling to admit where there has been dishonesty. Pointing the finger at others. Truth is ultimately freedom. Consider very carefully and seek wise council on how to restore trust and integrity and set yourself free.

EIGHT OF SWORDS

I USE WHAT RESTRICTS TO EXPAND.

This sword card is double edged, exploring the realm of powerlessness—feeling helpless and weak, as though no possibilities exist to influence a situation or relationship. This sensation can be all consuming; we become utterly bound by the restrictions of the mind, stripped of hope and agency. Yet, as with all Tarot cards—and life experiences—the possibility of transformation lies in the viewpoint and, more importantly, in our capacity to act upon what is revealed.

Feeling trapped can become the very force that initiates profound change. When the discomfort becomes unbearable and the pressure immense, something essential must shift. The card depicts a beautiful woman bound using the Japanese art of restriction, *kinbaku-bi*—the "beauty of tight binding"—encased within an upright Egyptian sarcophagus. Her serene expression suggests a conscious surrender, a transformation symbolised by butterflies fluttering around her head. Four swords are staked into the sand around her, like a ritualistic apparition, marking her internal journey. The other swords bar any possible exit point. Two vessels of spirit technology hover in the air at sunset—jewels of creative intelligence vibrating with potential.

This is the paradox: restriction on one edge and phenomenal liberation on the other. We often fall prey to whatever—or whoever—is imposing the limitation. But sometimes it is the limit itself that gives rise to focus, intensity, and ultimately, power.

When we remove every option except the path of fulfillment, we become laser-focused. By contrast, too much freedom disperses energy and weakens our ability to shape reality.

This insight is one I've explored continuously through graphic design, art, and life. Although the *Starman Tarot* appears rich with ideas and detail, I imposed strict creative limitations throughout the process. Despite having access to extraordinary tools—AI, endless references, and creative technologies—none of it mattered without the crucible of a single powerful idea. That idea must come from the great mystery, generating pressure. The entry point is always small, stripping everything back until only the essential remains—lean, strong, and meaningful.

To shape something alive with soul and emotion, you must take on the challenge, the risk, and the sacred duty of crafting the idea with care and purpose. Reliance on quick fixes or technology alone produces hollow results. It's discipline and constraint that refine the work into something authentic. And this applies not only to art, but to life.

Apply this same rigot to how you live—your time, relationships, and actions—and you'll discover that life, paradoxically, becomes easier. The practice of embracing creative restriction fosters clarity, energy, and flow. It seems counterintuitive, but by willingly leaning into difficulty, we activate true freedom.

This card invites you to examine the restrictions present in your life—not as limitations to be feaed, but as pressure points that can catalyse great ingenuity and directed purpose. Within what binds you may lie the precise shape of your liberation.

Reversed: Remaining stuck, unable to turn restrictions into creative fuel. Repeating the same patterns, trapped in endless overthinking with no progress. True transformation comes from taking small, consistent steps—day by day. This card invites you to identify the area of your life most in need of change. Visualise how you want it to be—feel the sensations, hear the words. Then reverse-engineer the path: brainstorm the actions, thoughts, and feelings needed to support that vision. Break them into daily steps and watch the restriction dissolve.

SUMMARY

EIGHT OF SWORDS:

The loss of freedom and choice, restriction, bound by convention and other people's rules. Honing the art of using the restriction as a ritual, a practice that carries the potential to give rise to a new perspective. It is narrowing options to arrive at the single point of power. **Reversed**: Remaining stuck, resentful of people and situations. Relinquishing the struggle and resting in what is. Discovering that freedom is a state of mind.

NINE OF SWORDS

I PERCEIVE DANGER EVERYWHERE.

There are times in our lives when we have a deeply disturbing experience that totally shocks our system, leaving us ungrounded, raw, frightened, and vulnerable to stressful feelings of pervasive threat. These feelings are compounded and easily triggered if we were on edge as a child, catalysed by an environment of insensitivity and threatening behaviour from major caregivers or role models. The card depicts a naked woman kneeling, hands clutching her head in terrible anguish. A dark, eerie, and ghoulish atmosphere pervades; large spiders crawl threateningly over her body, and a poisonous snake coils itself around her arm. Above her, the carcass of an ancient tree hovers, its branches contorting into the evil faces of witches and demons: a menacing, organic phantasm. Danger is everywhere, lurking in the shadows. It was the Swiss psychoanalyst (and mystic) Carl Jung who drew attention to "the shadow," that part of ourselves that is disowned, hidden from conscious awareness, and that stores the imprint of frightening and unacceptable experiences. These are then released from the unconscious into the content of our dreams at night, creating wild, bewildering nightmares that elicit fear, terror, anxiety, disgust, guilt, shame, despair or sadness, symbolic manifestations of the shadow. He proposed that the unconscious mind had a second, additional component not shaped by personal experience, called the collective unconscious, the reservoir of

material that has been inherited as a tribe, nation, and world being. It contains archetypal images with universal meanings such as those depicted in brilliant storytelling, mythology, film, theatre, art, music, computer games, and, of course, the Tarot, which, according to evolutionary psychology, relate to the natural instincts for survival: procreation, food, and shelter. According to Jung, dreams are a powerful way of acquainting ourselves with both the personal and collective unconscious and can facilitate the process of "integration," bringing all the parts of ourselves into equal relationship with one another rather than remaining denied, conflicted, and compartmentalised. This card suggests that you examine your psychological suffering, its mechanisms, and the projection of internal states into dreams and onto people and events in the outside world. Face up to fears by questioning if they are really true, and challenge any shameful feelings around family, sex and desire, underearning and success, appearance and visibility, worthiness. Understand that everyone has fearful disempowering thoughts and fantasies, and this is an amazing opportunity to question and clear the lineage of limiting beliefs that have been handed down through generations.

Reversed: Fear, worry, and paranoia are controlling you. Let art and symbols speak to the unconscious by using visualisation, drawing, writing, or a dream journal. Open and challenge yourself with powerful questions: Are these thoughts and perceptions true, 100 percent true? Familiarise yourself with "The Work" by the wonderful sage and truth teller Byron Katie, whose simple, tried, and tested method investigates the real truth of our thoughts and incorporates a "turnaround" that brings new facets of truth to light.

SUMMARY

NINE OF SWORDS:

The constant anxiety and torment of the mind, psychological turmoil, and a hyperactive imagination seeing threats where there are none, nightmares, phobias, and viewing the world as a hostile place. Often when we confront fears, we discover they are monsters made of nothing but vaporous thoughts that vanish in the light of inquiry. **Reversed:** Dominated by fears and worries, unwilling to question them. You are invited to challenge the validity of fearful thoughts: Are they really true? Can you know 100 percent they are true?

TEN OF SWORDS

I MUST EVOLVE.

This card is usually depicted as a person lying on the ground and being impaled by all ten swords, indicating sudden and unexpected failure or disaster. I have chosen a different visual interpretation. A blow from life is being delivered with immediate ferocity, and there is no way to avoid its full force. There is no time for pain or regret; in that very instant, we must accept full responsibility for everything in our life—our previous life perspective, context, has ended. Only then can we shed the skin of our old life and become master of our own destiny. As Pablo Picasso said, "Every act of creation is first an act of destruction." If in that instant of crisis we do not choose to take full responsibility, we fall back into the drift of life, battered and bundled by the fickle hand of fate. In the artwork, we are looking at the precise moment of choice—destruction and creation. Two figures—part man, part genie—are reeling from the surprise assault of falling swords. The one bleeding, dying from the many wounds that puncture his body, reaches out to touch the other, transferring his life force. The other figure is stronger, capable of defending himself, and, sending a bolt of energy, halts the impending fall of the sword. The genie essence illustrates the phenomenon that despite being magical, powerful, and able to grant extraordinary wishes, genies hide in the niches and nooks of the world, in lamps and containers, only to emerge for

people worthy and curious enough to find them. Similarly, our true creative power can remain hidden from ourselves and everybody else, locked deep within our mortal bodies and the patterns of our lives, never to be released. It is also a playful reference to Bowie's song "The Jean Genie" from the album *Aladdin Sane*, in which Bowie, having killed his flame-haired utterly fantastical Ziggy Stardust character, has given birth to Aladdin Sane, a much-darker, more dangerous, and streetwise character, adapted to survive in a decadent and sleazy culture. This card represents the sudden, unexpected jolt that pivots you between full responsibility and the drift. The key is to be ready . . . to be ready to choose responsibility and rebirth in that instant . . . the answer as always is practise and preparation. Give up the blame, complaint, the pointed finger, the moan and the groan; practice being response-able. When we claim our life for ourselves, we claim the power to change it into something extraordinary. We reframe the good and the bad as feedback edging us closer to our dreams.

Reversed: To remain damaged by your experiences, unable to use adversity to give rise to new possibilities. Blaming others for your misfortune, you forget that in pointing the finger, three fingers point back at yourself. Bad habits consistently realised, such as eating junk food, skipping exercise, drinking or smoking heavily, being unkempt, binge-watching TV, doom scrolling, too much sitting, isolating yourself, keeping poor company, or sleep deprivation, can all lead to a major collapse, signally that an entirely new approach must be birthed.

SUMMARY

TEN OF SWORDS:

The person you thought you were is destroyed by a sudden, shocking realization. Everything you believe to be true about yourself and your situation is no longer valid, and you are forced to give up the life you planned to have, the life that awaits you. You must evolve into someone more powerful and resourceful. **Reversed:** Remaining damaged by past experiences. Blaming others and the world. Know that you have an inner power and light that will carry you through and give you strength to make the changes you need.

CUPS

ACE OF CUPS

I OVERFLOW WITH THE ESSENCE OF LIFE.

The great joyful climax of celebration pours from the cup, after a sacrifice of time, energy, and comfort. It can be the union with self or another, the graceful sense of accomplishment and fullness after a long and arduous journey or project. Every drop of vitality has been used to reach this point. In the artwork, a beautifully crafted cup or chalice of gold and silver is present, overflowing with life-giving waters gathered from the clouds, ravishing and pure. The abundance of life-sustaining water, which heralds new life, cracks open the scorched clay earth below to reveal the hidden jewel of fecundity that lies beneath. Golden roots are nourished, growing, anchoring, seeking new intelligent pathways, and sending the twisted vines bursting into the sky and freedom. A lotus flower, sensual and exquisite, innocently blooms in the foreground, symbolising the purity that can be reached when we overcome the muddy waters of

attachment and desire. Out of the chalice rises a radiant woman fashioned from white marble, which also cracks open, revealing the liquid gold or abundance; within our being flows the miracle and mystery of life that allows us to shape reality. This card carries the energy of one who would sacrifice for the love of another, the love that can traverse harsh conditions and triumph even when it seems there is nothing left to give. The power to grow and flourish is released, the sacred milk of life spills over in celebration, and the richness of Being spills out. At last, the tide comes in, the replenishing water returns, and everything feels the surge of this peak experience. The ship that will carry us to new horizons arrives. The ecstatic pulse of existence rises and sweeps away negativity, cleansing you of the past sacrifices and discomforts, renewing you. This card communicates the energy of regeneration; that which has been fruitless can now bear fruit. Ideas that have required a tremendous amount of hard work and sacrifice can now be realised. Consciously open to receive this nourishing stream of calm, flowing energy into your life and seeing it birth new possibilities. This theme of regeneration is connected to the Fountain of Youth in mythological tales; the search for the spring that purportedly restores the youth of anyone who drinks its waters, thus becoming reenchanted with life, for it enlivens with creative potential. As life nourishes you, so you wish to give in return . . . offering your brilliance to the altar of love, a deep loving and appreciation for the life you have been gifted.

Reversed: Wasted energy; sacrifice and hard work in fruitless endeavours; the cup is emptied of life. Misplaced sexual energy leading to a loss of vitality and self-esteem. Creativity dried up, all out of ideas. Sipping of the Fountain of Youth becomes a compulsion to delay aging and the loss of beauty. It is time to reexamine your habits, routines, and daily rituals so that you can fill your cup with self-care and loving kindness, reconnecting with your inner beauty and radiance.

SUMMARY

ACE OF CUPS:

The pulse of existence that brings joy and ecstasy, exquisitely connected to every living thing, infused with love. You are open to receive pleasure and live in the beautiful flow of life. A great release of energy and vitality. **Reversed:** Addiction to bliss, constantly seeking ways to experience it. Ordinary life is dull; always looking ahead seeking the next hit. Connect with a structured practice that elicits fluidity of body and mind, such as vinyasa flow yoga.

TWO OF CUPS

I MERGE WITH THE BELOVED.

The human form carries amazing capacity for blissful expression, bliss so vast, boundless, and immeasurable that it encompasses every possible word or definition ever invented. Both tantra and Taoism teach that both women and men are gifted the capacity to be multiorgasmic, riding the waves of energy and pleasure to reach higher and higher peaks, opening and surrendering to one's true essence—the transcendental self—pure awareness—the Divine. This card reveals the beauty and power that is created when two beings, two threads woven together, unite. The art depicts the lovers in tantric union. Dynamic sexual energy supported by the power of intention, conscious surrender, and the skillful use of breath circulating through their bodies, received and given at their sex and their hearts, joining them in a unified circle of ecstatic colour and light . . . blissfully bursting through them and out beyond. They are sat incongruously next to a high brick wall, a hole through which reveals another reality—that which sits behind what is normally experienced, a recurrent theme throughout the deck. We see a stylised golden Caduceus, spiralling snakes, ancient sacred emblems of rebirth, winding around the staff of Apollo, god of healing. We see the dancing neurons to symbolise the astonishing interconnected, bioelectrical nature of Nature, atoms and molecules joined by the electric force; stars and galaxies organised and energised by

the same force. At the heart of tantra lies the idea of awakening kundalini, the "subtle" yet immensely potent spirit twin of electricity; a feminine, dynamic energy depicted as a serpent lying dormant at the base of the spine that can be awakened by cultivating sustained sexual energy and circulating it with loving presence, opening to your eternal and spacious nature. Preserving the energy release of the small, bodily orgasm, it is harnessed and shoots up the spine to the crown of the head to radiantly explode as light showering the body with the healing rain of love—ecstasies of the soul or consciousness—flesh and spirit, the same yet different in expression. This card, reflecting the lovers, invites you not only to look at the potentialities of sexual union outside in the world but also to travel within—to become more conscious of the dynamic dance, embrace, and play of the inner feminine and masculine energies that shape your life. Further, it seeks to make you aware of the potential dynamism and creativity that is birthed when two or more forces are drawn together—the union of entities or potentialities—ideas, talents, abilities, lovers, friendships . . . this in essence is a magical key with which to manifest and live a powerful, radiantly creative life. Whom you choose to spend your time with, exchanging ideas, feelings, and energy, will either greatly enhance your ability to make things happen or diminish it, so choose wisely.

Reversed: To be blinded by lust for another or lust for status; possessions can force us to compromise our deepest values, destroy our integrity, and engage in dysfunctional relationships. Giving our power away to others who don't have our best interests at heart, putting others on a pedestal, and mistrusting our own inner wisdom. Remember, we are only ever seeking feelings, a state of being: chasing after money not for the things it will buy, but for how those things will make us feel, and we chase after love or sex for the same reason. By getting clear about the core feelings we are seeking, we can find healthful, life-affirming ways to create those states.

SUMMARY

TWO OF CUPS:

The Divine accessed through focused sexual union, revealing the extraordinary in the ordinary. Seeing the interconnectedness of all things. You are the one you've been seeking. **Reversed:** Blinded by lust, obsessing over another person, putting others on a pedestal and seeking their love and approval. Letting everything else slide. Recentre, getting clear what feelings, emotions, and needs you are looking to another to fulfill and resolve. Sending love to those parts.

THREE OF CUPS

I AM HERE TO BE CELEBRATED.

Traditionally, this card expresses the joy of female friends meeting and raising their cups in celebration, precious in and of itself, but I wished to bring an additional dimension: the sacred journeying together through ritual. My wife, Esther, and I have long been fascinated by various guided practices that may involve modalities such as dance and movement, voice and music making, visualisation and breathing techniques. When we come together with a specific intention and use methods to release blockages while raising our energy and sensitivity, we open and access states that are heightened because of those present. There is a "harmonic resonance" as if lit by a flame; one person passes the fire onto another until the whole group is lifted to a new height and potential. So here we see three women kneeling, arms raised, in a state of ecstasy, surrendering to the golden elixir pouring forth from the three cups, showered with Divine essence. This all-encompassing energy is given by two gold-infused hands, suggesting that we are gifted transformation only when providence chooses—the possibility of ecstatic transformation being latent, just waiting for the right conditions to manifest. This Starman deck has many references—both symbolic and literally visualised—to the "elixir of life," and in particular its connection to gold and alchemy. The ancient Chinese believed that ingesting long-lasting precious minerals such as jade, cinnabar, or hematite

would confer some of that longevity on the person who consumed them, gold of course being especially potent, and its drinkable form appeared by 200 BCE. Whether its consumption produced long lives filled with ecstasy is questionable, but it was the American author and ethnomycologist Gordon Wasson with his wife, Valentina, who played a key role in bringing magic mushrooms into the public domain, claiming that they were the first Westerners to participate in a Mazatec mushroom ritual in Mexico. He was to write a cautionary note: "In common parlance, ecstasy is fun. But ecstasy is not fun. Your very soul is seized and shaken until it tingles." Indeed, historically, the intention of ecstatic experiences such as those who partook of the sacraments in the predominantly female Dionysian Mysteries was to produce a dramatic revolution and revelation in the self, to escape the confines of heredity and one's place in society and return to primordial nature, to be shaken free. The "economy of ecstasy" has recently risen in commercial hubs of entrepreneurial and technological activity such as Silicon Valley, where a growing number of professionals microdose on psychedelics to enhance focus and creativity. Coaches and trainers alike call upon a shared ecstatic state to move teams and individuals to new heights of performance and success. In many ways, the realms of ecstasy have been hijacked by the psychology of peak performance. Peak experiences shared create amazing bonds between people that can last a lifetime, a true sisterhood and brotherhood, and this card encourages you to explore that power of togetherness. It invites you to connect with the energy of shared celebration, to dance the great dance of life together—one movement—uni-verse.

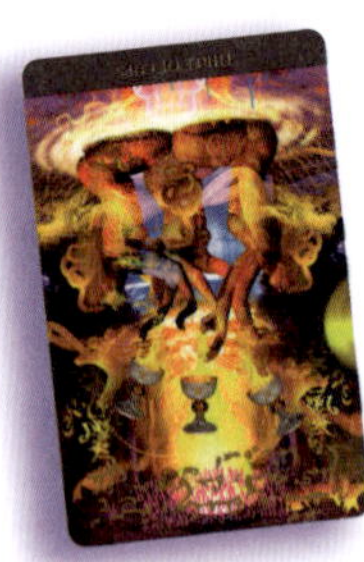

Reversed: Having no personal space, constantly at the beck and call of others. Becoming the martyr, always sacrificing your own needs for others, a group cause. Feeling disconnected, alienated; nobody understands me. Avoiding life through seeking addictive highs. Needing permission and affirmation from others, not trusting your own feelings and needs, self-expression, intuition, and autonomy. It is time to carve out your own "me time," attending to your own remarkable vessel of consciousness. Explore ways to nourish and honour yourself on your journey through life. Build life-affirming rituals into your daily existence and consciously reconnect with practices and activities that have brought you joy and aliveness as an adult, as a teenager, as a child. Celebrate yourself.

SUMMARY

THREE OF CUPS:

The joy of giving and receiving, sisterhood and brotherhood, creating sacred space together. Touched by grace, something miraculous is living through you. Time for gratitude and deepening relationships, friendships, and connections. **Reversed:** No space for yourself, always busy and occupied fulfilling other people's needs. Unable to truly give and be cherished by life. Carve out nonnegotiable time to pursue your own creative gifts. Treat yourself to something that lifts your spirit.

FOUR OF CUPS

I AM HURT AND POISONED BY LIFE.

One of the founding fathers of personal development, M. Scott Peck, in his groundbreaking book *The Road Less Travelled*, begins with an opening sentence: "Life is difficult." When I read this decades ago, it was a revelation; someone else of authority was admitting how tough life was. He goes on to say that once we fully understand this and accept it, life is no longer difficult. Through the process of seeing clearly and accepting what is so, we transcend it; the difficulty no longer matters. Many teachers, before and since, have shared this simple yet profound observation; nevertheless, we are still deeply shocked when we come face to face with the difficulty, sadness, disappointment, and loss, the plethora of challenges that life serves up to us. Often we act as if life is purposely tormenting us, working against us, goading us, and blame others for the circumstances we find ourselves in. Feeling victimised, we then punish ourselves for not being good enough, that seed of self-contempt and misrepresentation that was often born and perpetuated in childhood, the ill-conceived projections of floundering adults. Too often, survival is then accomplished by not playing in the game at all, thereby avoiding any chance of getting hurt by not participating in life, like a ghost, watching from the sidelines. In the art we see a figure crouched despairingly in a pool of thick, black, viscous liquid, head in hand, overwhelmed by life. The colossal hand that is floating above him is from a bronze statue of the Roman emperor Constantine, who purportedly brought an end to the persecution of Christians during

the Roman Empire, suggesting that the persecution and torment of thoughts and past hurts can indeed end. Above him, the two upturned cups pour dark misery, saturating him with woe. The same chalice that disperses the golden elixir can also spill dark misery just like we ourselves can. Like the cup, our self is essentially clear, neutral. When our egoic false self, which has long adopted the culturally entrenched pattern of strife and the fight for survival, chooses the supposed context, the lens that colours and frames an event, life often becomes toxic. Our cup is filled with self-recrimination, guilt, shame, and regret—stacking the evidence we've been collecting since childhood. However, should we create a new context, the cup can be filled with clear fresh water, or a golden elixir. The teacher and leadership master Werner Erhard reminds us once again through the teachings of Socrates that if what you experience as "you" is not satisfying, this is clearly not "you." Self as self is complete, satisfied, fully accepting of what is, without any stories and drama. This card then suggests that you re-create the context for your life so that you can fully receive its blessings. You no longer need the point of view that has seemed so real, so uncomfortable, living life as a "problem." There is much to be grateful for; the four cups can hold fresh sparkling waters should you choose. Emotion, the motion of energy through you, can be seen for what it is, without the "story." Accept those difficult feelings and sensations and let them pass through you. When we become a curious observer, we can open to something new. Before, the point of view created you; now you create the point of view.

Reversed: Remaining trapped in the stories your mind creates, always dissatisfied, life is one long complaint with no possibility of creating a new viewpoint. This could be an opportune moment to begin challenging the stories you have blindly accepted from the environment of your family, school, further education, workplace, local community, country, culture, and beyond. Refresh yourself with the stories, aspirations, and hardships overcome by those people you admire. We live in an incredible world populated by great thinkers and teachers past and present. There has never been a time when wisdom teachings from a myriad of cultures and perspectives have been so generously offered and freely available. Sample their message and recommended practices, noticing which ones your mind-body system resonates with. Release the torment; ritually cleanse and rebirth yourself into "beginners mind."

Summary

Four of Cups:

The guilt, shame, and regrets that hover over us, turning life toxic and painful. But we are invited to realise that we are not those thoughts and feelings; they are energies travelling through us. It's only when we take ownership and hold on to them that we stop their flow in and out. This is the natural flow—in—out. **Reversed:** Avoiding responsibility, victimhood, and blame. Unwilling to break the spells that cause misery. Realising that the most powerful medicine is bitter; admit your role in the drama and receive the healing.

FIVE OF CUPS

I AM INCONSOLABLE.

The Swiss American psychiatrist Elizabeth Kübler-Ross, a pioneer on near-death experiences and the process of grief, postulated that there are five stages of grief: denial (This can't be happening), anger (Why me? It's not fair!), bargaining (If only . . . I would), depression (Why go on?), and acceptance (It's going to be okay). Although toward the end of her own life, she said that the stages were not always a linear, predictable progression, she opened the door for us to understand that grief is a process that unfolds across time. Ultimately the process travels across different emotional topographies and must make the full journey in order to reach the land of acceptance and integration. In this card, a distraught figure stands by the river, as a hand—maybe a loved one—desperately reaches out from the rushing torrent, swept away. A mystical, winged Pierrot, the sad clown, looks at the scene unfolding, clearly concerned yet fascinated by the spectacle of such biting sorrow. It highlights how the ubiquitous torrent of media keeps so many captivated by the spectacle of other people's misfortune. However, the five cups mirror the five stages that must be ingested and integrated in order to move on and ultimately heal. The red inflammation of three of the cups, the emptiness and meaninglessness of one, and then hope, a return to the heart, in the last. For this card to have impact, one does not have to be dealing with something

catastrophic. It points to the fact that we all carry tremendous grief: ancestral grief, family grief, cultural grief, grief for our loss of innocence. We all live out the five stages of grief in numerous ways: A dream job we have worked so hard for falls through; a relationship breaks up; children leave home. No one can pass through life untouched by grief and loss. In seeing that grief is part of the natural cycle of life, we can stop fighting against it and allow ourselves to feel what needs to be felt. The Tarot offers us an opportunity to see ourselves through different eyes, to see what needs to be questioned, healed, and released. It offers us new vistas to move toward and explore. As with the Four of Cups, we have the capacity to create a new context or viewpoint through which we can explore our pains and discomforts, whereby they can be transformed into something wondrous. Byron Katie's system called "The Work" offers a way of questioning and releasing the painful stories we inhabit, stepping into the open freedom that is our true, radiant, untarnished self. This card took me to my own deep grief: the loss of loved ones, the failures, the hard times that I had put my family through with my relentless pursuit of creative dreams. The fast-flowing river in the card has more than one meaning or possibility. Of course we can be swept away by the river of tears, but we can be cleansed by it too. We can put right what we can and let go of our grief, let it be taken back into the great ocean of life. For me, this card does not point to the arrival of some form of grief, for it has already arrived and we carry it in our cells. Instead it presents a question and a powerful possibility. It asks you to look at the grief you are holding on to. It invites you to complete with it and let it go, letting life—Nature—take care of transmuting it back into vitas, energy.

Reversed: Thrust into a sacred realm where the healing capacity of emotions is allowed to work. Moved to use the force of grief as a force for good. Let your bodily instincts carry you through the turmoil, trusting that you can survive your emotions. Take a deep breath and listen to yourself from the toes up, noticing the sensations travelling through your body as you navigate this new emotional landscape. Take your time; there is no rush or right way of passage; trust one day at a time. The cup is carved deeper by emotion that tears at the heart of your being, creating more space to hold wonder, joy, and grace. Deep compassion and empathy.

Summary

Five of Cups:

The great river of tears. Swept away by grief and sense of loss, abandoned by the power and presence of meaning. Life feels like a constant struggle leading nowhere, which no one truly understands. We all are navigating the great river of life, and the waters can either sweep us away or flush us clean to live fully again. A choice sits between these two options. **Reversed:** Thrust into a sacred realm where the healing capacity of emotions is allowed to work. Moved to use the grief as a force for good. Deep empathy.

SIX OF CUPS

I AM IN WONDER OF LIFE.

To be able to wash all the responsibilities and problems of life away and return to a time of innocence, a time when the days stretched on forever, and the complex burdens of adulthood were inconceivable, carries a strong allure. Life does not work that way, and even if we reach back into childhood and step into our young shoes once more, we will be ignorant and innocent; better to go forward, wise and innocent. Innocence fused with ignorance is so delicate. A small child sees a plane in the sky and interprets it as a giant bird; it is beautiful. But this type of innocence will be lost; touched by time and the world, it cannot last; we must go forward. Understanding and awareness can dispel ignorance and kindle a fresh, mature form of innocence. We discover something lovely: innocence flavoured with wisdom. The artwork depicts a woman swathed in graffiti, a tribal-patterned catsuit reaching out to catch a golden star floating elegantly in the air. On the floor a tiny girl stands patiently to also catch a star, mirroring the image in the painting above her, while the shadow of a young boy joyfully leaping to seize a star is cast across the wall. Hung on the purple wall of the gallery, there is a gilded, luxurious framed picture of another woman; surprisingly, she is dressed in black rags, worn, impoverished by life. This scene represents those of us who are tarnished by life, reaching out to touch the golden, pristine beauty of the stars. It speaks of those who have travelled so far away from innocence; yet, despite the harshness of life, they see that the beauty of innocence is still possible—alive. The woman in black has already

touched a star, and it has turned into a dark star; its innocence—so fragile—is lost. There are more, though; another chance will come. She reaches for another. The shadow of the young boy expresses the utter fragility of innocence, so joyful and so fleeting. The tiny girl reminds us that we cannot stay as we were; we must grow. There is sadness in this artwork, a yearning to once again be untarnished, and yet, there is much hope; the cups are ready to receive. The art gallery—art—can rekindle a sense of fascination, play, and joy. Through art we can express the world-weary mind in soft, vibrant colours, transporting others to that place, that vibration of purity and perception, leading them into it. The cutting edge becomes a gentle line of colour. This card moves you to reconnect with simple embodied forms of expression, infusing what you create with the lived flowing wisdom of your life, moment to moment. All young children are artists, free of self-judgment, bathed in the delight of mark making for its own sake. Likewise, I have seen even truly withered spirits brought back to life through the simple joy of art, of hand stroking paper. Ultimately, your life is your canvas, your experiences—your actions—are the colours, shapes, and patterns, your wisdom the paintbrush and the dexterity of your hand. Take a little time and carve some space in your days to simply play. Draw, paint, shape. For many people, confused, isolated, and in fear, cut off from friends, family, and colleagues during the COVID pandemic, making art became their redemption. Draw, collage, paint, print, or sculpt your deepest fears and confusions; release them onto the page so you can see them. Allow your creative spirit to reimagine and refine them, portals to your deeper consciousness, inner light, and acceptance. Visualise your dreams, potentise them as graphic totems—show yourself what your heart dearly yearns to express. Life will come at you; it is relentless. The teacher Byron Katie calls this relentless(ness) Love. Life will keep coming until you see things clearly as the open space of awareness, true innocence.

Reversed: A yearning to turn the clocks back keeps us stuck in fantasy. Unable to employ our wisdom to move forward, the world is just too harsh. A strong desire to return to the holding protection and innocence of the womb, forfeiting the process of living, the hard-won trials and lessons of life. To be a fully integrated adult is an art, requiring openness, curiosity, and the willingness to learn and accept what is. It is never too late to express something beautiful and meaningful.

SUMMARY

SIX OF CUPS:

The desire to go back to a time of innocence and simplicity. Seeing with fresh, untainted eyes—excitement and joy. Softening. Discovering that you can flower and ripen instead of growing old. The ability to be free of resentments and blame, both to embrace and consciously create the path leading to a beautiful future. **Reversed:** Reluctance to grow up and master the role of a powerful adult. Stop! It is never too late to say yes to life!

SEVEN OF CUPS

I USE MY IMAGINATION.

This is the card of imagination. For the iconic shaman and philosopher Terence McKenna, the imagination signalled the presence of a Divine Spark within human beings. He saw our imagination literally as the descent of the World's Soul into all of us. There is no part of our humanity that isn't impacted by the imagination. We are a spark of imagination, and Mother Nature does not create things that have no use. Life viewed through evolutionary eyes reveals that Nature shares her resources incredibly sparingly. The question then arises, Why do we have this faculty that allows us to conjure and manipulate realities that do not exist? Imagination can be "looked at" as a vast extension of the visual faculty. Our minds have a spectacular multidimensional eye. In the artwork, the character's physical eyes are covered, but we are gifted a window into what he is seeing through his inner eyes. We are offered a window into a whole other reality. Out of each hovering cup there arises a spectral image: the human head, symbolising the mind or the ego, which can either guide with wisdom or become self-obsessed and irrational; the bat, symbolising the power of vision (inner and outer); the mask, symbolising the personas or masks we all wear, deceptions; the mushroom, symbolising our symbiotic relationship with other earthly life-forms; the lightning bolt, symbolising spirit coming to earth; gold coins, symbolising wealth and abundance; and the star geometry, symbolising structure and creativity. The most obvious place where imagination offers the highest value

is in the domain of human creativity. The activities of producing art, architecture, creative writing and poetry, music, theatre, and dance can be seen as the fingerprints of imagination: they are the evidence of its touch. It's as if the imagination leaves clues everywhere to show where it has been. Unlike a thief, who is careful not to leave fingerprints, imagination wants to be discovered; it wants us to know that it is right here in full view. This card calls you to explore your imagination fully, to delight in the fact that you can imagine at all. If you look, you will discover a paradox: It is impossible for you to imagine not being able to imagine. As we move ever more into a domain of virtual or "light" realities, the intractability of physical matter is no longer a restriction. We can build anything our minds can entertain. Here the fingerprints of imagination are algorithms instead of canvas, clay, or physical movement. Imagination is effectively the new currency of these light-based realms. Importantly, there are always blessings and burdens. With fewer and fewer restrictions upon what we can create, the issue of morality takes centre stage. More than ever, the imagination must be used skillfully to enhance our human experience and preserve the animal and plant kingdoms. Thoughts that can instantly be shared with millions can lift us to new heights, inspire, and entertain: They can also evoke fear, prejudice, and violence. Will we create endless perversions or miraculous vistas? The answer is probably both. When your mind projects fear into the world, tremendous damage and unhappiness can be the result. The acronym FEAR—false evidence appearing real—is a powerful prompt, a reminder to bring awareness and robust questions to bear on life situations around you. Bring new vistas to life; make them tangible with love. Use your imagination with wisdom; cocreate with the World's soul.

Reversed: Imagination running wild—seeing fear and danger everywhere. Believing imagined stories without questioning. Paralysed by too many choices, letting others or algorithms decide for you. Despite the endless hype of technology, millions are trapped in its dark economy—underpaid, undervalued, feeding the "miracle" machine. Consider a technology detox: go into nature without devises. Give yourself the powerful gift of reconnecting with your true nature and the slower rhythm of the Earth. Stay focused on your well-being, seek out beauty, and recognise its presence.

SUMMARY

SEVEN OF CUPS:

The ability to innovate and conceptualise. Receiving guidance from dreams and altered states. Experiencing things differently and knowing that there is so much yet to be discovered. Delighting in the power of the imagination, being a channel for new ideas and ways of understanding. **Reversed:** Living in a fantasy world, inability to question what you are told is true. Seeing danger where there is none. Take back your power; unplug from the stream of negativity.

EIGHT OF CUPS

I SEEK ANSWERS TO LIFE'S BIG QUESTIONS.

The term "vision quest" was first coined by nineteenth-century anthropologists to describe the rite-of-passage ceremonies of certain Native American cultures, usually undertaken by boys approaching puberty. Certain preparations were made before the initiate spent a period of days alone in his chosen place in nature. Often fasting for the duration, he had to overcome challenges and fears in order to receive wisdom and guidance from nature and the spirit world concerning his purpose and how he might serve his tribe. He received this in the form of symbolic messages in the physical world and through dreams. They can be viewed both as personal and collective events that are guided and witnessed within the community. The idea of venturing into the wilderness, removed from the routine activities and duties of life, to sit in sacred space, quieting the mind and heightening the senses to travel deeper into the nature of self and existence, is probably as old as humanity. In the artwork, the young man holds his head in sheer bewilderment, when faced with the task of gathering the wisdom held in each cup. As one cup flies away, the flames of another lick the fuse of dynamite in its neighbour. A cup spurts noxious green gas, and he is about to unwittingly kick over the cup filled with liquid gold, and on we go . . . This card very much reflects where I was at when I created it: Ideas were flying away from me, and some important documents I needed were locked away in a security-encrypted folder. I had a fever and had to think about an art piece that was needed urgently, people were getting

heated, tempers were fraying, and I was about to lose a significant amount of money as a result. Just to cap it all off, I discovered a huge patch of green mould in my office, which kicked off billions of toxic spores as I removed it. And that's just how it is some days. We must venture into the wilderness of our lives to gather wisdom. Just by virtue of being born, we are thrust into a vast, paradoxical, beautiful, and infinitely complex wilderness. The important takeaway is that we must, from time to time, take ourselves off to unfamiliar parts and be challenged. We must leave behind our comforts and routines to connect with the wilds of Nature. Conversely, the cities we inhabit and the tasks we are called upon to do are also Nature. Our lives, just as they are, constantly offer us guidance, wisdom, and healing. For the most part, we are just too busy or preoccupied to stop and take note, receive the learning, and allow ourselves to be transformed into a more effective and heart-centred people. In my case, in relation to this card, it was art and life converging to tell me to take care of my physical body, deal with problems as soon as they arose, and call upon experts to deal with problems I could spend a month of Sundays trying to resolve. This card suggests that there is much wisdom and guidance to be gained wherever you are, if that is your intention. Creating sacred space to sit in Nature, away from the habitual rhythm of life, may also be very valuable; as the *having* and *doing* fall away, the *being* is left. In this culture we are conditioned to do the exact opposite: to focus on what we must *have* materially in our lives and to *do* the work to manifest it to *be* happy. Focus on the quality of "being," follow the signs, and stay alert to what life is communicating to you.

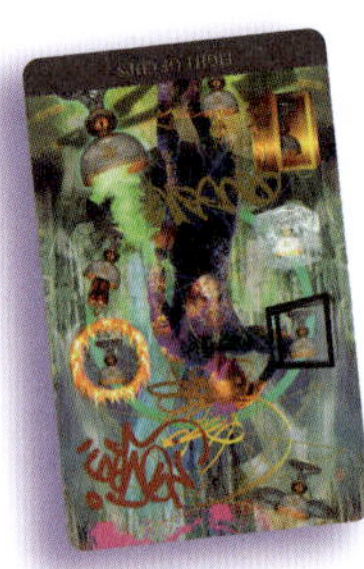

Reverse: Constantly seeking, restless, and misguided. Unwilling to risk journeying to uncomfortable places, facing up to the truth of what we have become as a result of our actions and choices. Lack of self-love and compassion, neglect of physical body, and little discipline to still a racing, confused mind. Take a deep breath; there is plenty of grounded healing available when we know where to look. Consciously cleansing yourself will be a valuable pathway to remove the toxic overload of demanding thought: bringing high-quality "clean" water into your daily life, using a distilling machine, reverse osmosis, or local spring, and why not research and commit to a short simple fasting protocol such as juicing fresh, organic vegetables? Bathe consciously, honouring your body. Connect to the restful healing powers of rivers and babbling brooks, and the rhythm of the ocean waves; life is on your side.

Summary

Eight of Cups:

The vision quest, willingly venturing into the wilderness to be tested and transformed, communing with the elemental wisdom of Nature. Seeking answers to important questions. **Reversed:** Constantly seeking, restless and dissatisfied, lacking spiritual support and guidance. Orient yourself to a meaningful cause that brings good things to many.

NINE OF CUPS

I AM LAVISHED BY THE GOOD THINGS IN LIFE.

For this card I absolutely wished to say goodbye to the portly, middle-aged man depicted in traditional Tarot and to create something that I felt truly expressed the exuberance and delight that this card needs to communicate. I wanted something celebratory, sexy—radiant. Everything about this card for me is about being fully immersed in the pleasures and beauty of life. There is a strong sense of completion; the kind we feel after achieving something significant and worthwhile. There may even be a sense of resolution, of having lived one's destiny, that if life were to take you away right now, you would be satisfied. We can enjoy the spaciousness, weightlessness that opens, feeling great euphoria, ripples of delight streaming through our nervous system, utterly visceral. We simply radiate . . . and people can feel it: the sympathetic resonance of joy and fulfilment. When we feel complete, we become fully embodied in the present, our senses alive and expansive, the mind open and clear. In the card we see a woman seated, languishing on a curvaceous avant-garde sofa, raising her cup and inviting us to toast her success. Her cup holds the golden likeness of the Buddha's hand in Gyan mudra, the energy seal that stimulates the pituitary gland and is known as the mudra of knowledge, concentration, and expansive creativity. The other cups stand like exquisite plinths hosting an array of geometrical light archetypes, the

geometrical language of nature and building blocks of life and creation. They are also symbolic of the underlying metaphysical principle of the inseparable relationship of the part to the whole. The principle of oneness that permeates the architecture of all form in its astonishing diversity. The golden/magenta sphere behind her, floating amidst the incandescent sunset over gentle water, is the universal symbol of unity, wholeness, and completion, divinely feminine, the motherly womb of spirit. For many who read the Tarot, this is the ultimate "wish fulfilment card"; for me it is something else entirely: the "Declaration" card. Wishing is a fundamentally different reality, defined as feeling or expressing a strong desire or hope for something that cannot or probably will not happen. Instead, evoking the potency of Declaration, you no longer report about the conditions or environment needed for something to happen; rather, you create the conditions and the environment. You DECLARE who you are. You DECLARE what you do. You DECLARE what you create. Something is brought into existence the instant you declare it to be so. This card then signals a sea change for you. Asking "why" instead of "how." When you have a compelling reason to make something happen, the question of how is no longer the issue: how is merely the next step you take toward your goal. This way of living will free up a phenomenal amount of energy; you become the open space in which the next action arises. Your words have power because you do what you say without reasons, justifications, and excuses; complaints disappear because there is a natural joy in being totally responsible for your life and what you create. With the energy of this card, we also discover that like the lizard, we can be regenerated; we too possess untapped powers to regenerate, grow a stronger body, a stronger, more joyful psyche, and stronger connections and relationships. Life is abundant, and it is your natural birthright to fully enjoy the fruits.

Reversed: The reverse of this card can manifest as arrogance and a lack of empathy for others, especially those who are struggling in life. Tendencies to overindulge, becoming addicted to hedonistic pleasures while everything else falls apart around us. An aversion to challenges; you just want to roll with the good times. You are "intoxicated" by life, stupefied, markedly diminishing your physical and mental control. Wake up—it's time to get to the gym and clean up your act! Regular physical training (without your phone) not only releases the mind and obviously strengthens the body but also connects you to a new, healthier community. Remember that the fates gifted you your birth and life circumstances; act with humility.

SUMMARY

NINE OF CUPS:

The experience of attracting good fortune wherever you go, expecting and receiving the best, life lived as a celebration free of guilt and regret. You have the power to manifest and enjoy every aspect of your creations. **Reversed:** Overindulgence, lack of understanding and empathy with people's everyday concerns. Inability to face challenges and evolve. Reach out and help someone.

TEN OF CUPS

I EXPERIENCE THE JOY OF LOVING CONNECTION.

There is something exquisite and miraculous about journeying with fellow travellers on this road called life, that we are not alone. Loneliness is a great deprivation and one that, in the face of divorce, increasing mobility, and an aging population, is becoming more prevalent. The people in our lives offer up reflections of ourselves, like some great fractal, different facets of ourselves are revealed, and contrasting edges of our character flame into existence with another personality, another energy—life-giving and life-sustaining energy. When we are alone, our needs remain unseen and unheard, our stories unshared, and we lose ourselves in the vastness of thought and the emptiness of four walls. Only now is loneliness "coming out," being seen to be the great premature killer that it is. And so it is that we can be incredibly thankful for all the people who show up in our lives . . . service providers, neighbours and colleagues, community members and friends, and, if you have been so blessed, the families we have. This was one of the most poignant contrasts for our family in Bali, with little room for loneliness when old and young live altogether in extended family compounds, and the all-year-round warm weather encourages meeting outdoors. We see a family in the cards, within a bejewelled circle of cups that seem to burst with golden light, one with the essence of full-spectrum light. Cups, as we know, represent the element of water, and

visible light is the only part of the electromagnetic spectrum that refracts in water, which led to the evolution of the first appearance of eyes millions of years ago in the vast oceans of Earth. The exotic environment reflects the rich, diverse abundance and interconnectedness of life, inviting you to become aware of how everything is in a dynamic conversation with you and inviting you to participate. A mother and father with their daughter, who looks set to make her mark in the world, are being showered by a gentle golden light from the cups above. The family cat gives the scene a familiar air, communicating embodied sensuality and an independent nature that is just as happy chilling in the sun. This card invites you to take time to connect with special people in your life, those you love and have travelled with for some time. Acknowledge their presence in your life with fresh eyes; experience their beauty, their courage and fortitude, and their wisdom, feeling into and through their stories, to fathom their radiance. Everyone around us is a gift, a reflection. Everyone around us is a teacher, showing us where we get caught in the web of judgment and self-righteousness, of separation and ignorance. If we would only give ourselves more moments to experience first the joy of loving connection with ourselves and then turn to the other, to give love and appreciate the miracle of their existence. The family that birthed and grew you and the family you intend to create for yourself are realms of incredible possibility when you choose to let them guide you to become the best version of yourself. To love and enjoy your family, you must first accept them as they are, accept yourself as you are, and then invent ways to touch and be touched by their lives, letting old ancestral patterns fall away. Pick up the arrows of judgment, blame, and dysfunction and transform them into flowers of love, gifting them to yourself, your family, and the world.

Reversed: Losing connection with yourself, loss of freedom and independence, no high-quality time to recharge your batteries. Abandoning your dreams, constantly pleasing and taking care of others and feeling resentful. Continuing the line of dysfunctional ancestral patterning where the dynamics of family were toxic and possibly unsafe. Notice the tools that each member of your family uses to get attention and their needs met. Look at your own. Lack of love and intimacy begins at home with yourself—into-me-see. Commit to a daily practise of self-care, of putting your needs first for a change, attending to yourself, cherishing yourself—out of that well of well-being, then, other facets of life can flourish.

SUMMARY

TEN OF CUPS:

The emotional security and sustenance of a home nourished by beauty. Family . . . tribe . . . togetherness. Learning and creating together, sharing abundance. Taking time to listen and support those around you. Together we all rise. **Reversed:** Losing yourself, loss of freedom and independence, abandoning dreams. Realise that you must put on your own oxygen mask first; make self-care a priority.

ACE OF PENTACLES

I CAREFULLY TEND THE SEEDS OF SUCCESS.

In the *Starman Tarot* the Ace of Pentacles is about the remarkable potency of life. Moreover, it explores the breaking down of elements to become the nutritious soil out of which new growth and fertility arise. The raw components of your life, especially the painful and difficult times, become the compost and fecund soil out of which a stronger, more resilient and "alive" you can be created. When you excavate the past for stories that are negatively charged and reframe them so that a positive spark can be released, the catalyst of learning and renewed potential is born. We revisit the "story" and break it open to entertain another possibility or viewpoint, which can then seed itself and grow your being. My intention for this card was to express the wonder that we have the incredible potential to grow and become someone else—that things occur in our lives that catalyse a whole paradigm shift, symbolised by the cat and its nine lives. The artwork expresses the utter wonder of growth, where the seed must appear

to destroy itself, tear itself open, in order to sprout a tender new shoot. The woman represents the surrendered self that must appear to be destroyed; broken open in order to flourish. The books in the soil signify that knowledge must also undergo the same process—for example, science must take what was once believed true, investigate it, take it apart, and regrow into a more advanced and complete answer or new hypothesis. In this card the impossible project is seeded—the most incredible venture you can imagine can be nurtured. All astonishing accomplishments come from humble beginnings, energy and resources that are consistently gathered and attended to. We are reminded that when we are working toward a powerful goal or mastering a skill, even when it seems as if no progress is being made, so much is still happening below the surface of our awareness. This is an amazing card for connecting creativity with abundance, expanding the human mind to the cosmic mind through the ancient art of plant medicines and adaptogens. This ancient plant realm that was seeded 470 million years ago, far more ancient than humans or animals: Does it serve us, or do we serve it? Just as the seed of life, this planet is birthed from stars, so the *Starman Tarot* was seeded by many diverse experiences, encounters, and synchronicities, and my work with Bowie. The buried books contain my notes from when I worked with Bowie on the *Earthling* project, the ideas broken down into the soil from which this new form has grown, and in turn, this too will become the soil for something else to come into being.

Reversed: While it's important to create a strong intention to manifest something, one also needs to locate the necessary resources and the right conditions for it. You can't sow seeds in fallow soil; projects of substance take time to nurture and mature. In life, we only ever seem to circle around one or two major themes, and like the spiral we have the opportunity to revisit them over and over again. Review your ideas and plans and know there is a right time for everything.

SUMMARY

ACE OF PENTACLES:

The stage is being set for great things to come. The potential is in the seed, which will grow into a new vision or way of being. Noticing the magic of Nature, connecting with the power of herbs and adaptogens to make you strong and vital. Establishing good habits that help you grow and learn. **Reversed:** Planting your seeds in fallow soil, plans that never materialise, misguided timing with too many ideas. Be systematic, seek advice, check your timings and resources, and make a real commitment.

TWO OF PENTACLES

I PERFECT THE ART OF BALANCING RESPONSIBILITIES.

At the core of the *Starman Tarot* there sits the deck's trickster nature, who plays with the traditional representations of the Tarot, turning things on their head. In this spirit, I often fashion the earth out of the sky and the sky out of the earth and enjoy pushing the boundaries of how the characters are visualised and the environments in which they find themselves. Traditionally, the character in the Two of Pentacles is depicted juggling two gold pentacles bound by a ribbon or chord, which forms a lemniscate, the infinity symbol. The character is placed firmly on smooth, solid ground, while two sailing ships are wildly tossed around on a volatile sea. This forms the story of his solidity as the chaotic and shifting world transpires in the background. However, I wanted to catch my character in a time slice as he surfed the sky on an "infinity board." He is solid and sure in his own capabilities, particularly the foundational skill of balance and the volcanic eruption behind him—the volatility—which is unable to shake his confidence. He is earthed, but not as we might expect. He is intrinsically motivated, has immense body awareness, and has married internal energy work with physical movement. He has learnt how to align his body and centre his awareness, allowing him to respond rapidly to any change in his environment. He is a master of his art and knows that he can adapt to whatever comes his way, recognising that in a state

of flow, he is not moving; rather, he is being moved. His adornments are in balance; everything is playing out perfectly for him. He rides upon infinity, the symbol of things constantly in perfect repetition, representing the harmony of reinvesting your material gains into your gifts and passions—investing your past experiences to ensure your continued wisdom and growth as a human being. The cycle is never ending; everything in the universe is reinvested; beneath the appearance of chaos sits perfect harmony and balance. At the root of your own life sits the same harmony; everything recycles and is renewed in each moment. When faced with change, the turbulence of events that might be presented at times in life ride the wave of disturbance by maintaining practices, interests, and relationships that nourish and support your core strengths and priorities. In any moment, you can centre yourself with the power of the breath, helping you feel calm, present, and focused, to respond rather than react, allowing your natural state of balance and composure to be restored. Riding the waves of life, we learn to let go of the drama and, returning to equilibrium, glide steadily on.

Reversed: Feelings of fear and overwhelmingness, unable to cope with uncertainty. As a result, there is a real rigidity in your behaviour, trying to control things that you have no power to control. Addictive coping strategies may very well surface as you seek to control other aspects of your life. Aversion to healthful risk means playing it safe and missing the opportunity to learn and grow. Investigate a "grounding movement practice" such as 5Rhythms dance, chi gung, yoga, Pilates, or tai chi to bring your attention away from the frenetic mind into the calm wisdom of the body. Bodywork such as massage, cranial sacral therapy, and reflexology will also assist in releasing tension. Know that it will serve you to surrender and accept the circumstance you find yourself in, and instead to turn inward to discover a way out.

SUMMARY

TWO OF PENTACLES:

The ability to deal with change, the skill of prioritising, adapting to different situations and people, finding the perfect balance between action and assessment. Trust that you can handle whatever comes your way. **Reversed**: Unable to cope with uncertainty, inflexible of mind and body, playing it ultrasafe. Out of balance personally and professionally. Use yoga balance postures such as the Tree or Warrior to regain this sense of balance, equilibrium, and strength.

THREE OF PENTACLES

I RELISH CREATIVE ENDEAVOUR AND COLLABORATION.

This card refers to the passion, sheer aliveness, and embodied intelligence that comes from doing something well, mastering a skill set. Traditionally, someone aspiring to become a master of a particular trade would begin his journey with an apprenticeship, followed by employment as a journeyman before finally reaching the status of self-employed master craftsman. To achieve anything of real note and value, we must dedicate our time and resources to learning and growing our knowledge and skills. In the card, we see the artful central character balanced upon the three golden pentacles, symbolising the dedication and risk involved in applying oneself to something that isn't easy. Despite Malcolm Gladwell's infamous proposition that it takes 10,000 hours to master anything, it appears that the evidence was misconstrued, and the issue of mastery is far more complex, influenced by factors such as age, genetics, and internal motivation, as well as practise. Not everyone, it seems, is destined to become an expert in a given area by putting in the time. Deliberate practice, constantly pushing oneself beyond one's comfort zone, developing particular skills through training activities designed by an expert or coach, and getting feedback so that weaknesses can be worked on and improved are ways to evolve a talent, but even that accounts for only 25 percent of those who succeed at becoming experts in a chosen field. Repeatedly practising the same set of skills in the same way leads to roadblocks; strengthening the same neural

pathways may increase your brain's neuroplasticity in one regard, and the skill becomes more automatic, but ultimately to improve an ability we need to keep adjusting the execution of it to get closer to our goal: quality, not quantity. Visualisation or mental practise, the cognitive rehearsal of a physical skill without movement, is additionally an incredible tool to facilitate success. In fact, research has shown that a combination of physical practise and mental practise requires half as much physical practise as does physical practice alone to reach the same level. It appears that the same areas of the brain are activated in both activities. Meditation can also be helpful in clearing the mind, enabling it to be more receptive to new ideas. In the artwork behind the labyrinth sits a visual from one of the notebooks I used when working with Bowie on the *Earthling* album. They serve to remind me of the heartfelt dedication and hard work that was required of me: the research, acquisition of new technological skills, a whole new scale of project management, and, above all, the intention to astonish myself and others. Creativity and the work of creative endeavour are the passion, discipline, and perspiration required to bring something unknown into existence, a burning curiosity and desire to resolve something that is not whole or in balance within the psyche, which needs to be expressed to become whole. When we apply ourselves with intense concentration, our everyday worries dissolve, as does our fear of failure, with no space for doubt. This card suggests that you are in your creative flow; freely exchanging knowledge and ideas, giving and receiving feedback, scheduling and planning, collaborating with others to bring something of value to fruition—a rich flowering, engaging both the left and right brain simultaneously. Adopting the exquisite balance of process (presence) and result (focus) leads to overarching success, well-being, and wholeness.

Reversed: There is a fine line between vocation and obsession, and a danger in crossing it. Obsession, the addiction to control and perfection, leaves no space for anything else to show up in life, generally resulting in isolation, self-neglect, and loss of balance. When all our eggs are placed in one basket and it's knocked over, broken, everything is lost, and our lives are devastated. Self-care must be an integral part of any creative endeavour, developing the physical and mental resources for sustained effort. Similarly, to pursue a vocation requires the steady evolution of meaningful work and study.

SUMMARY

THREE OF PENTACLES:

The passion, sheer aliveness, and flow of doing something well. Being seen as the master possessing the discipline and dedication to do something extraordinary. Taking the time to hone your skills so they become second nature. Don't be afraid to aim high. **Reversed:** Obsession, isolation, and self-neglect in pursuit of an idea, not capable of sharing your talent. Break this pattern: reach out to others in the same field and share your passion.

FOUR OF PENTACLES

I HAVE GREAT INFLUENCE AND POWER.

Life is dynamic, constantly in flux. No matter how desperately we want our life circumstances to remain stable, we must accept that we are powerless over the force of time. All the material things, skills, and wisdom we have worked so hard to acquire are in effect only borrowed—we cannot take anything with us when we die except the essence of love. In the art, the character is lavishly adorned; gold sits around him. His face is covered, but the dualistic head represents the different faces he wears—identities; there is another behind him. As time goes by, we often take on more identities, more roles through jobs, family, friendships, and other responsibilities. Most spiritual practices offer methods to let go of the identities we take to be so real, to see clearly that what we think of as "ME" is simply a collection of ideas, beliefs—patterns of behaviour—essentially not real. In the card, the heads appear to be fragmenting and breaking apart, which illustrates the idea that our personas are indeed ephemeral. The ability to let go of beliefs and patterns of action that do not serve not only us or others, but also the other forms of life that inhabit our planet, is a blessing. Additionally, the capacity to reinvent oneself and acquire new beliefs, becoming a more functional, knowledgeable, and generous human being, is also a blessing. As the scene unfolds, the eye—the eye of life—simply observes the dynamic movement and exchange of

energy. The drama playing out in the card is ambiguous. We cannot be sure if he is reaching out to collect the floating heads—a new identity—just above his hand or if he is letting them go, just like a floating lantern, back into the expanse of sky. So, we are left with two meanings: that he naturally attracts good things to him, so all he has to do is reach out and take them, or, conversely, that he has a taste for freedom and wishes to let go of accumulating. Both options carry positive and negative possibilities. There is something supremely wonderful and life affirming about prosperity—manifesting the beautiful experiences and material possessions you desire. However, as time passes we can become laden with belongings, properties and wealth, expectations and beliefs. Life can lose its edge when we never have to strive for things, or we can become addicted to the feeling of constantly needing more and more to fill something that feels missing. This card therefore suggests that there is huge confidence and ability to leverage all that you want out of life, but that when it comes too easily, something is lost; we lose touch with reality. We touch only the sides of life, missing out on the expansive range of emotion and feeling that connects us to the hard-won successes and strife of others. However, there is much to be gained when you have the command of ideas and resources that go beyond the personal and extend to a noble cause that can impact the well-being of many.

Reversed: When surrounded by abundant wealth and riches, it's easy to succumb to fears of loss, a paranoia that it is going to be taken from you. There is a loss of gratitude and connection with life, the lack of recognition that everything is interdependent. In the natural world, no organism is cut off from its surroundings. Secrecy and a misguided refusal to share can lead to crippling isolation and hoarding. Money and assets are ultimately a medium both of exchange and storage. This card suggests that it's time to explore ways to meaningfully exchange energy, channel your resources to a worthy cause, and let new life in.

SUMMARY

FOUR OF PENTACLES:

The command and prestige of having resources and ideas that are impactful. But there is a realization that the only true wealth is in sharing what you have acquired to enrich people's lives and ultimately the world. Prosperity is a lived experience; it's dynamic and cannot be held. Who do you want to become? **Reversed**: Arrogant refusal to share, isolation and paranoia. Unhealthful need for security and secrecy, corruption. Channel your resources to a noble cause.

FIVE OF PENTACLES

I AM DESPERATE AND DESTITUTE.

We can go through life unaware that astounding beauty and miraculous things surround us, right there for us to reach out and touch. We rush past a beautiful flowering tree, completely oblivious to its rich and fecund display. We bicker with those we love, unaware that this moment of aliveness, of being conscious in this life, is so fleeting and precious. So many fail to see the wonder that sits within their grasp and thus experience the poverty of unawareness, lack—lack of time, lack of support, lack of money and resources, when in reality there is no lack—just a lack of awareness. I am reminded of the wisdom story of the beggar sitting on a box by the side of the road, begging for thirty years until a passing stranger suggests he open it, only for him to discover that it is filled with gold. In the artwork, the two characters are crouched begging for money and food, positioned in front of a Garden of Eden. They were outcast from paradise and yet are separated only by a slender barbed-wire fence; it is well within their reach. The two realities exist side by side, but from the place of lack they are blinded to the possibility. The figures are slowly disappearing into the graffiti-covered boards; soon they will recede from view, becoming just another part of the mean streets. This card invites us to look for our own disowned treasure while also referring to the very real hypocrisy and unfairness that the world offers up. Misery

and suffering sit alongside vast wealth and opulence. The millions upon millions of people who must survive and support their families on so little, while others have so much. Inequality, isolation, segregation, and ignorance play out around us every single day, and we must decide how we wish to be in the face of this. One of people's greatest fears is to be cast out of their homes, their families, their tribe and to have to live on the street, impoverished. The fear can compel people to generate riches at any cost, while others remain caught in the trap of poverty, unable to escape. It can keep you trapped in a fruitless relationship or move you to create extraordinary things and help many others along the way. The Five of Pentacles invites you to consider your own relationship with the issues of poverty, inequality, and unfairness. It also suggests that you acknowledge and actively seek out the phenomenal abundance all around you, feeling it as part of your own being. Travelling to various parts of the world that live in tremendous poverty and experiencing a lack of bitterness and open generosity, while, conversely, living in one of the wealthiest parts of London and witnessing such a lack of generosity—life traversed in ungainly SUVs, imprisoned behind high walls and closed gates—made me deeply question my own fears around poverty and isolation. To live with an open heart and generous spirit, no matter what, is a powerful practice, one that carries the possibility to transform the world we experience.

Reversed: This card indicates that there is tremendous strength and wealth of spirit to be gained through adversity and hardship, when one is no longer dependent on possessions, the trappings of success or status, to live well. Becoming extremely resourceful, creative, and able to appreciate the many tangible and intangible blessings in life.

SUMMARY

FIVE OF PENTACLES:

The denial of basic needs, excluded and deprived. Poverty and struggle, ignored and powerless. Cast out of the tribe, shamed, worst fears realised. Not able to see that true wealth is right at your fingertips; the currency of life is the energy you bring to what you do. **Reversed:** Becoming strong and resourceful through adversity and hardship, no longer dependent on possessions or status. You transcend normal limitations.

SIX OF PENTACLES

I HAVE MORE THAN ENOUGH.

At the time I started working with Bowie, my design partnership of five years was practically bankrupt. A passion-driven desire to create designs that were innovative and pushed boundaries, compounded with a scarcity of willing, adventurous clients to commission us, had chomped through all of our resources. The bank had run out of patience, and an unexpected bill from the tax office had cast a death sentence on the business. The axe was expected to fall in seven weeks, the time between the final demands and the administrators showing up like the grim reapers. I had just finished this unpleasant calculation when the phone rang—a small, rather tedious design brief was being offered, just enough to call a stay of execution for a little longer, but there was no joy in my heart to do it. That same night at home in Islington, I dreamt that a tall tiger creature—a strange and wonderful power totem—came to me. It was surrounded by flying serpents and glowed with spectral turquoise and pinks. Every time it opened its arms, I was showered with gold. In the dream, I asked it what I should do, and the reply was two words: CREATE ART. On a rational level, this just didn't make any sense—I was poised at a financial precipice, and yet, at once it was the only thing that made sense. All doubt about the path ahead was evaporated by the brilliance of that dream. The next morning I cancelled the boring job, cleared the

decks, and set about creating the kind of art and designs that filled me with joy, excitement, and aliveness. As destiny would have it, it was these designs that were to feature two months later on the front cover of *Creative Technology*, a copy of which stirred Bowie's imagination on a flight to the States and prompted him to call me. His art and musical projects, which positively hummed with his spirit of innovation, opened the door to a vast creative vista and generously rewarded me for my art and design. This sudden transformation of fortune also gifted me the opportunity to direct the flow of abundance, helping other aspiring designers and artists to shine and prosper. There are times when we must move past our fears and step into a universe of trust—trust in the natural flow of abundance. Remember that there is never any shortage of resources; they simply need to be channelled in the right direction. In essence, our job is to fully show up and be seen, present and aware that what we have to offer is *enough; we are good enough*. When we are full with life, *have enough*, people are intrinsically drawn to us, sensing the expansive quality of enoughness; there is no request or demand being made of them. In that spaciousness, we then move and inspire people through what we do and how we are in life. I have discovered that when we become intensely interested and intimately involved with life, it becomes intensely intimate and involved with us. When we can generously offer life our very best, just for the natural joy and aliveness of it, life begins to offer us the very best back, almost always in unexpected and delightful ways. I invite you to see how this card can help you step into the flow of resources and the generosity of others.

Reversed: The reversed card signals misdirected resources, throwing money at things rather than presenting well-thought-out solutions that have everyone enrolled. Financial aid that encourages corruption or dependency rather than activating local assets and forging independence. The old Chinese proverb "You give a poor man a fish and you feed him for a day; you teach him to fish and you give him an occupation that will feed him for a lifetime."

SUMMARY

SIX OF PENTACLES:

The custodian of abundance, directing the flow of resources to those in need. The ability to support and deliver a worthwhile vision, philanthropy. Take a step into a world that is alive and receptive to your positive energy and generosity. The more value you add to people's lives, the more abundance you will receive, and around it goes. **Reversed:** Misdirected resources, encouraging dependency, overprovider. Teach people; help them to grow and prosper from their own talents.

SEVEN OF PENTACLES

I WILL CONSISTENTLY NURTURE MY LIFE VISION.

The suit of Pentacles is traditionally associated with manifestation and material wealth, while a broader interpretation of wealth is one in which it's kept in the three treasure chests: the body, mind, and spirit. This card is all about nurturing a vision: a beautiful rose grows from red-hot molten lava, up through a hole in the scorched earth skin, complete with its own ecosystem in miniature. It grows because it has been tended and lovingly willed into existence, regardless of the obvious impossibility. In my own experience, I have seen that the things I thought were impossible became possible through small consistent steps. Focusing intently on perfecting that next small step while simultaneously never losing sight of the greater vision, the "why," the raison d'être, adjustments are made along the way—each action grows out of the previous action. Like the miraculous process of growing a baby—just two cells multiply, through the simple consecutive process of doubling, into the two trillion cells that make a human life. The gardener pictured, gentle, accomplished, dedicated, and above all supremely patient, possesses the magic touch of bringing things to life in the most hostile of conditions. Life too can present hostile conditions out of which we must grow and nurture a vision of ourselves. Many do not pay exquisite attention to the details and fail to nurture their young, tender life force: opportunities don't sprout and

possibilities remain buried. In the distance we see the magical beanstalk leading to a mystical city in the clouds, representing the exponential growth of intelligence into the "clouds" and beyond. Intelligence that now resides in the ether has grown incrementally out of the binary-numeral system that was invented over three hundred years ago, developing from analogue to digital to atomic—eventually to spiritual technology—and back home to the epicentre of god. In us, consciousness moves in one great circle, from pure energy, to atoms, to single-cell entities, to multicell organisms, to self-consciousness, to superconsciousness, and back to god consciousness. The potential exists to move from ignorance to unity through the vessel of life, understanding that life must be nurtured with the seeds of good habits, for a radiant future, right now. This card indicates that your vision of life must be nurtured. The situations and circumstances may not be ideal, with few skills and resources, but with consistent, tender-loving care and pruning, they will grow stronger and see daylight; the delicate shoots of ideas and possibilities will flower. Draw your fellow visionary gardeners to you, distancing yourself from people or situations that stunt your growth, and invest in learning new skills and knowledge. Every one of us deserves to grow rich meaning and purpose out of the soil of life.

Reversed: Lacking the patience and the due diligence to attend to your creations and relationships in life. More haste means less speed; rushing around busy often achieves very little other than survival. Oversights are made, and we must begin again. To thrive requires a sensitivity to conditions, loving care, patience, and light—bring these qualities to yourself. Know that having a "B" job to support and sustain your lifestyle is perfectly sensible, provided that each week you set aside high-quality time to attend to and grow your creative shoots; otherwise the dream is in danger of being lost or forgotten.

SUMMARY

SEVEN OF PENTACLES:

The patience and tenderness required to grow things of value and beauty, sustained effort, willing to accept nature's cycles, delayed gratification. Refusing to be rushed, taking a stand for the very best outcomes. Ecology and respect for resources. **Reversed:** Feeling undue pressure to make things work, punishing deadlines, the fast economy. Slow down; don't live life like it's an emergency.

EIGHT OF PENTACLES

I AM DOING THE WORK I WAS BORN TO DO.

This card sets out a crystalline landscape of minerals with many facets, in which a character is seen standing on a golden elegant structure, fashioning and refining the elements of some exquisite space-time sculpture. Robotic, made of intricate parts and connections but still in human form, it is clearly absorbed and attentive to the task at hand. If this was a human being, perhaps an artist, we might assume that he was in a state of "flow," completely absorbed, honing and perfecting his skills, creating a meticulously detailed piece of work that expressed something essential about his existence. We may be able to delegate tasks to artificial intelligence or robotic forms with robust efficiency, but to be conscious of the process of creation may well remain a uniquely human phenomenon. To take on something intrinsically valuable and use our range of intelligences keeps something crucially alive in us. Education that socialises us for the world of work has traditionally focused on external rewards and merits rather than internal, intrinsic motivation, and this will have to transform if we are to encourage people with flexible skill sets and knowledge to work across different disciplines and collaborate in valuable, unique ways. This card invites you to look deeply into your world of work and review those projects and moments where you felt most alive, inspired, capable, absorbed, and joyful. This card invites you to look at where you

need to apply yourself fully and feel the joy in the doing of it—of doing it well and to your fullest competency/capacity. In the card, the character has many characteristics of a robot, and yet, it still maintains a human form and is clearly infused with purpose. I'm playing with the possibility that no matter how much we may become "enhanced" beings, the sense of our own corporeal existence will be seen as a treasure: our consciousness is a mind/body consciousness, living light, unique and precious. If you have neglected your physical form, this card is calling you to use it and fully experience it, the miracle of agility, dexterity, and strength. If you have neglected to stretch your mind, you are being invited to expand your intelligence and knowledge, to investigate, listen, and research, and to think critically and offer solutions that touch the lives of others. When you are willing to put in the real work to bring something about, it "enhances" your innate sense of being; you become absorbed in life, living on purpose.

Reversed: Doing work that is repetitive and dull or that you actively dislike but making no plans to change. Merely focusing on external rewards and finding no pleasure in how they are created. Lacking discipline due to boredom, mild depression, and constantly being distracted from important tasks. Stop wasting your time; you deserve more, and the world deserves more of you. Turn your A job into your B job. It's time to explore and investigate the passions and interests you had as a child and teenager, and as a young adult, and begin the process of researching career/business opportunities. Discover more deeply what your friends are up to, and your friends of friends—use your networks wisely.

SUMMARY

EIGHT OF PENTACLES:

The honing and perfection of skills that bring immense satisfaction, meticulous attention to detail, commitment to the highest quality. Careful choice of materials and techniques. Creating things of value and use. **Reversed:** Lack of application and dedication, work as a means to an end, fear that it's just not possible to thrive doing what you love. Revisit your interests and passions; actively explore how they can grow into a bigger possibility.

NINE OF PENTACLES

I AM IN CHARGE OF MY DESTINY.

A beautiful woman stands in an ancient and magical chamber, the scene of countless long-forgotten rituals, filled with abundant treasures. Intuitively I chose a bat to be present, striking away from the mythological preconceptions that associate bats with night, darkness, and evil. In China, for thousands of years there has existed a deep love and respect for bats, regarded as the masculine principle that feasts on the feminine fruit. The Chinese word for bat sounds identical to their word for good fortune; consequently, many of their legends associate bats with good fortune. Happening across a group of five bats would represent, for example, the five causes of happiness: wealth, health, long life, virtue, and natural death. European folklores tell us that washing our face with bat blood will enable us to see everything with great clarity. Bat blood could also be used to enhance a man's virility, firing a woman's passion when placed under her pillow; a bat bone in your pocket would ensure good luck. In the card, the bat appears to be delivering one of the golden pentacles to the woman, illustrating that good fortune is being gifted to her: she naturally receives what is good. The falcon sits upon her arm, symbolising vision, freedom, and generosity. Falcons were used at the funerals of Egyptian pharaohs, viewed as intermediaries between the divine, eternal heavens and the mortal earth. In a very real sense, we all possess the

power to see into other realms through dreams and our imaginations, and for us to manifest anything of substance, we must first imagine or dream it. Everything is born out of the womb of the nonmanifest to arrive in your imagination, be received by it, and coagulate into thought forms. You can take charge of your destiny and what you think you deserve to experience in this lifetime. Through your inspired belief, focus, and continued earnest effort to nurture and grow your fullest potential with patience, you are now ripe. You have been designed by Nature to naturally flourish and ripen into this delicious fruit. You have earned this badge of mastery and accomplishment fuelled by the intrinsic rewards of doing what you love with great talent and skill. Stand and receive the recognition and acknowledgment; your success inspires others, and like the fruit, the lush vessel that forms to disperse the seed, the next generation is motivated. This card therefore invites you to think beyond limitations and live outside the borders and restrictions of what you are told is possible. Ask yourself, what would be a truly amazing experience to manifest for yourself right now? Be receptive and connect to the matrix of flow and abundance, the dynamic, expansive principle of life.

Reversed: There is a sense that you've missed your mark, that you will never realise your potential. An overbearing feeling that you're not good enough, that you can't make it. And even if you are standing at the top of the mountain, you feel like a fraud, unable to relax into your destiny. We are here to remind you that it's never too late to be great! It's never too late to dream and let life help you make it a reality. Let life live you.

SUMMARY

NINE OF PENTACLES:

The natural harnessing of resources, easily attracting opportunities, connected to the matrix of abundance that is life, fullest potential being realised. Seeing that life is a dynamic conversation: the more you engage with it, the more it engages with you. **Reverse:** Feeling that you're not good enough, that you can't make it, that you're a fraud, unable to relax into your destiny. Let life live you; you are a conduit through which life loves to flow, so open up and allow it to flow fully.

TEN OF PENTACLES

I GIVE A WEALTH OF LIFE-SEEDING IDEAS.

We see a beautiful apparition in the sky: a goddess of molten gold and light, an emissary of astonishing knowledge and bringer of wondrous riches. A magickal tree laden with mystical fruits sits at the centre of the mysterious vessel that she travels in, as giant gold nuggets are drawn from the earth to hover in the air. Gold and platinum are the precious metals forged by the extraordinary heat generated by a violent collision of neutron stars. Created when giant stars die in spectacular supernovas, the cores of neutron stars collapse, allowing protons and electrons to meld together to form neutrons, producing small yet incredibly dense stars. The mystery of how to create gold, which so occupied the alchemists of old, has been found to be this fallout, scattered by dying stars. Recent space research has revealed that humans share most of the same elements that are common in the universe, hydrogen being the most abundant. We also share oxygen, carbon, and nitrogen; the proportions are merely different. To add to the magick, there is gold in your brain too—inside every neuron there are just a few atoms of gold that keep the neuron charged, keeping you thinking, moving, and feeling alive. Just as our minds are never at rest, our bodies are never static but are in a constant process of renewal, not fixed at all, more like a pattern or a process. As dynamic beings, we must exchange energy to remain alive, like all living things. Wealth, then, in the

largest sense is ultimately created through dynamic relationships. The concept of "six degrees of separation" is the theory that any person on the planet can be connected to any other person through a chain of acquaintances that has no more than five intermediaries—emphasising the hidden manifesting power that sits at our fingertips. Similarly, the spiritual teacher Byron Katie—creator of a system of inquiry known as "The Work"—suggests that we could have anything we wanted if we were prepared to ask a thousand people. Once we are open to the idea of networking, of building, maintaining, and refining networks, of collaborating and facilitating each other's visions and dreams, anything becomes possible. True wealth comes from consciously creating high-quality experiences regardless of circumstances—we don't play the wait-and-delay game of *when . . . then . . .* "Living alchemy," then, is the process by which the basic, raw materials of your life, both good and bad, can be formed into the gold of experience. The artwork depicts a little alien family gliding to Earth on a giant golden pentacle, arriving in a new land, a new domain to explore and create together. This card invites you to cocreate, explore with those you love, reach out to those that inspire you, and share and actively enroll the world in your vision. Discover the wealth of experiencing life fully with others. The whole of humanity is your family. The whole of planet Earth is your home; focus on the diverse abundance of life.

Reversed: Weighed down by a physical inheritance, property that doesn't suit your purposes. The burden of too many possessions all requiring upkeep and storage. Not enough energy to appropriately disperse them, trapped in consumption. Vision is buried. Let go of what's not needed. However overwhelming, all the "stuff" of life is in your environment. It's time to get organised and begin the process of clearing, one room at a time. Try the three-box system: a "yes" box, a "no" box, and a "maybe" box; alternatively, use Marie Kondo's method of releasing everything that doesn't spark joy. Remember, it is memories that are valuable, not things. Be generous and reestablish the networks that will support this next phase of life.

SUMMARY

TEN OF PENTACLES:

The future sustained through a new wave of heart-centred, people-centric ideas and innovations. Passing on your knowledge and wisdom to the next generations. Planting trees that you will never sit under the shade of. You are part of something bigger. **Reversed:** Trying to hang on to possessions that no longer serve you. Weighed down by old beliefs that keep you stuck. Lacking a higher vision. Let go of what you don't need. Lighten your load. Pick a domain to add value to.

YOUR TIME TO SHINE IS NOW

The world is shifting; consciousness is evolving. This process heralds astonishing possibilities to bring ideas to life and for all of us to live in our communities as wise, fully expressed human beings in service to a greater principle. As we traverse this boundary between the old and new ways—two aspects of being?, contexts of reality—we are faced with increasingly difficult choices and challenges to navigate. It feels as if everything is dramatically speeding up, becoming more chaotic and unpredictable. Times of great transition will always be accompanied by a sense of confusion and less control over our lives, our work, our finances, and our families. But within, truly amazing opportunities are available if we are willing to embrace this time as an invitation to become the alchemist of our reality, where every challenge contains the seed of a new possibility.

Having the tools to surf the wave of this evolution is what will ensure you have the power and momentum to keep creating new realities moving forward. The ability to understand and take charge of your mind, be able to control and calm your nervous system, stay in vital health, and remain resourceful and energised amidst this change is more important than ever before. Not just so you can navigate and prosper through the challenges, but so you can be of loving service and value to your family, your friends, your fellow workers, the spiritual community, and all the people you interact with. To be in your highest creative power and expression in difficult times means you can become a conscious participant in the new world and consciousness that is being birthed out of our current one.

To be a powerful creator is to experiment and learn from your experiences, glean wholeness and wisdom from Nature and the wider world, and be open and receptive to an inspiring vision of what your life has to offer. It is time to reimagine and transform the chaos in your own mind and, as you do so, transform the chaos in the world. As we travel together, committed to a sacred, spiritual path, a tribe of conscious creators using the power, wisdom, and guidance of the *Starman Tarot* alongside the resources we offer via our website (talks, workshops, master classes, etc.), we will literally bring a radical new context to life.

All the problems and conflict we see in the world arise from a systemic ignorance of our spiritual light nature, and the sanctity of all life. When the astonishing truth of who we are is not only alive in the mind but also fully embodied, an inner joy spontaneously arises. We are no longer fragmented and adrift in a meaningless world. When that inner joy and reverence for the astonishing diversity of humans, animals, plants, fungi, bacteria, and the mineral realms are present, of life itself, you are gifted the opportunity to operate from that frequency of being—a powerful state—regardless of circumstances. You are a vital conduit of life, part of a greater story that is unfolding in miraculous ways.

Drawing on the light that animates your entire mind and body, becoming more open and aware of the inner stream of joy and the calling of your evolving consciousness, you will naturally shine and radiate resilience and hope. You will be a vital testament

to transformation through how you live your life and embody the core message and possibilities that emanate from the *Starman Tarot* and the resources we offer, and, indeed, all the wisdom teachings and people who also carry this message. You become the healing balm to someone's fear and worry, or the answer to someone's question to the universe. "*How can I realise my creative gifts, let go of fear and limiting beliefs; how can I no longer succumb to the demands of the small, anxious self?*" As you evolve, you become the inspiration and example of what it means to rise above the cultural tide and embrace a new level of radiance.

We (Davide and Esther) have been blessed to walk this path of transformation for many decades and bring incredible things into being—even some seemingly impossible things. It has enriched our lives and opened incredible vistas to explore and share our experiences. Together, we have traversed numerous challenges, some formidable setbacks, and failures. We are still very much learning and honing our abilities and deepening our understanding, often humbled by how much we still must learn. However, we fully embrace and live the quest to bring more beauty, love, freedom, and wonder into the world. We live to share the energy, gifts, and vision that we have been granted; it infuses our daily practices, rituals, work, and relationships and has become our natural disposition.

The point is that we didn't begin with this amount of passion, purpose, and knowledge. We didn't have some rarefied angle on life or bountiful resources to work with. As an old shamanic saying goes, "You come into this life with two books; one is already written and the other you get to write yourself. The question then becomes, How can the one I get to write be the most inspiring, adventurous, and meaningful?" The *Starman Tarot* and the contexts, deep questions, and possibilities it shares are the flame that ignites the energy for something more magickal and compelling. Here there is a wonderful paradox; when you realise that the vision isn't yours, the vision can come to life in its full glory, and in the same way, when the magick is just about you and not in service to the Light Intelligence—the Great Mystery—it doesn't work. Metaphorically speaking, when you consciously plant trees that you will never sit under the shade of, you are granted access to the energy and interconnections that are normally hidden from view.

So, in this spirit, we would be honoured for you to be part of this movement. It is no accident that you have found your way to this material and its potent invitation. We invite you to join us as part of this exciting creative tribe travelling together on this mind-blowing adventure. We encourage and embolden you to become part of a community that fervently supports one another to live fully creatively expressed, leaning into their greatness and sharing life's magick together.

In Love and Radiance,

Davide Esther

Davide and Esther De Angelis

THE NEXT STEP

We feel sure that you will use the *Starman Tarot* for your personal evolution and elevation for years to come and will stay connected to this energy, key to sustained transformation. Diving deeper into this living alchemy will help you reconnect to your own innate wholeness and inner radiance while being encouraged and inspired by your fellow travellers. Below is a list of key resources for you to utilise, many of which we offer for free.

To begin with, why not subscribe to our mailing list to receive powerful weekly news and ideas, access to bonus products and trainings, workshops, talks, and other opportunities to meet and work with us in person, including consultancy. Visit: www.DavideDeAngelis.com.

You will also gain instant access to Davide's free master class, Tarot and the Miraculous Secrets of Light, where you will discover how to align with the creative energy of the Tarot and have a dynamic, intimate conversation with the Universal Light Intelligence. To receive it, visit www.DavideDeAngelis.com.

ABOUT THE CREATORS

DAVIDE DE ANGELIS

Davide is a visual alchemist, Tarot creator, and visionary teacher whose work traverses the realms of art, futurism, and consciousness. A best-selling author and explorer of fantastical ideas, he channels his artistry and wisdom into works that awaken the soul and ignite imagination.

As the creator of the internationally renowned Starman Tarot, with its extraordinary fusion of mysticism, shamanic art, and design inspired by his seven-year artistic collaborations with David Bowie, Davide invites seekers on a journey of insight and self-discovery, exploring the mysteries of existence through breathtaking visuals and evocative storytelling.

Bowie described Davide's work as "Potent Visual Alchemy," encapsulating his ability to conjure symbolic energy, beauty, and meaning through his work.

Davide's books, including the psychedelic sci-fi novel The Seed and the spiritual odyssey The Guiding Principle, invite readers into astonishing dreamscapes and higher realms of possibility.

As one of the original pioneers in digital art and graphic design, Davide has collaborated with companies such as Apple, Virgin, and Sony, and Bowie himself, producing groundbreaking album art, fine art, interface design, and projects that blur the boundaries among design, philosophy, and science.

In harmony with his creative work, Davide channels his energy into mastering jump rope routines, playing the didgeridoo, and creating rhythmic worlds with wild percussion. He's passionately immersed in the frontiers of plant and light nutrition, physical regeneration, and amplifying vital energy.

Moved by an insatiable curiosity and sense of wonder, Davide has traveled the world, immersing himself in the art, cosmologies, and ancient mysteries of diverse cultures, alongside many years of training with shamans and energy masters. He has devised and facilitated transformative retreats, vision quests, innovative learning systems, and master classes. Davide's art and teachings open expansive vistas of creativity and self-realization, inspiring others to live with boundless energy, passion, and purpose.

www.davidedeangelis.com

ESTHER DE ANGELIS

Esther is a visionary artist, living radiance coach, creativity catalyst, author, and speaker, whose vibrant energy and passion for transformation light up everything she touches. She is also a raw-chocolate alchemist, musical improviser, and funky mother.

With over fifteen years of experience teaching her unique form of chakra yoga across the UK and Europe, Esther has devoted her life to exploring creativity and human potential. She is the founder of the Free Smiles Movement, which has shared the simple yet transformative power of a smile with thousands.

Dance is at the heart of her work. Her signature practice, Dance Radiance, blends yoga, shamanism, artistic expression, and therapeutic wisdom into a holistic journey of awakening. Through this practice, Esther has guided thousands to reconnect with their inner intelligence and unlock their full vitality.

A true creative force, Esther holds an MA in fine art and has a background in theater. She has embraced diverse mediums, from ceramic sculpture and printmaking to digital montage and carnival arts. Her dazzling hand-painted Art Cars, adorned with mystical realms and cosmologies, bring art to the streets with breathtaking impact. Esther made history by creating and leading London's first-ever renegade Art Car Parade.

While living in Bali, Esther designed Chakrita, a stunning fashion line of beachwear and dancewear that celebrates color, sensuality, and empowerment. Women worldwide have been inspired to express their passion and dreams through her visionary designs.

Driven by a thirst for adventure and wisdom, Esther has journeyed across the globe, immersing herself in the arts, spiritual practices, and philosophies of diverse cultures. She has spent over two decades delving into esoteric traditions with master teachers of Kabbalah, Buddhism, and shamanism.

Esther's mission is clear: to flood the world with radiant color, boundless creativity, and the transformative power of joy.

www.liveyourradiance.com

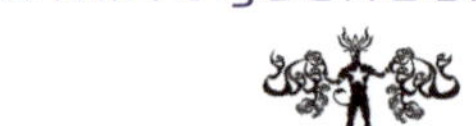